ISBN 978-1-5284-7058-2
PIBN 10084660

FB &c Ltd, Dalton House, 60 Windsor Avenue, London, SW19 2RR.
Company number 08720141. Registered in England and Wales.

CIVIL GOVERNMENT

IN

THE UNITED STATES

BY

GEORGE H. MARTIN, A.M.
SUPERVISOR OF SCHOOLS, BOSTON

REVISED EDITION

NEW YORK ·:· CINCINNATI ·:· CHICAGO
AMERICAN BOOK COMPANY

MAR. CIV. GOV.
W. P. I

PREFACE.

THE attention of teachers is invited to the five distinctive features of this book: —

1. *Its full statement of principles.* A knowledge of these principles will be found of value not only in studying our own institutions, but also in studying ancient and modern history. They furnish a standard by which to test the various governments that have existed, and often explain the influence that those governments have exerted.

2. *Its comprehensive plan*, embracing the state, county, city, and town organizations, as well as that of the United States. As every citizen takes part more directly in the local administration than in that of the general government, he needs to understand the powers and relations of the state and municipal governments.

3. *Its historical method.* The endeavor has been to show not only *what* our free institutions are, but *why* they are, by tracing their development from germs in the early English constitution through the colonial and revolutionary periods of our own history.

4. *Its topical arrangement.* The teacher will find this a help in assigning lessons; and the scholar, in studying and remembering them.

5. *Its omission of details.* A school text-book on this subject should not be a compendium of political statistics, nor an office-holder's guide, but a citizen's manual.

The features outlined in the foregoing extract from the preface to the original edition of this book are retained in this edition because they have given the book its distinctive character and been the cause of its success.

The present edition brings the book up to date by embodying all recent constitutional and statutory changes, and by selecting illustrations of a timely character.

Any text-book needs to be supplemented by use of legislative manuals and reports, municipal registers and ordinances, and by such records of public proceedings as current newspapers furnish.

The historical portions of the book are intended to aid the student in answering the "questions for thought" which any wise teacher will propound, but which it is not the province of a text-book to supply.

CONTENTS.

PART I.

PRINCIPLES OF CIVIL GOVERNMENT.

PART II.

CIVIL GOVERNMENT IN THE STATES BEFORE THEIR INDEPENDENCE.

CONTENTS.

PART III.

THE CONSTITUTIONAL GOVERNMENT OF MASSACHUSETTS.

PART IV.

THE CONSTITUTIONAL GOVERNMENT OF THE UNITED STATES.

PART I.

PRINCIPLES OF CIVIL GOVERNMENT.

CIVIL GOVERNMENT IN THE UNITED STATES.

CHAPTER I.

DEFINITION OF TERMS.

THE word "govern" is derived from the Latin *gubernare*, meaning to steer, to pilot, and then to guide, direct, control. To govern, therefore, is to control, and government is control. Thus the divine government is the control exercised by the Creator over his creatures. Family government is the control exercised by the head of a family over its members. School government is the control exercised by the teacher over the members of the school. When a pilot would guide his vessel from one port to another, he must know what courses he may take, he must choose one of these, and he must have the means of compelling the ship to take this course. These three things — intelligence, will, and power — are necessary to all control, and therefore to all government.

Government.

When the controlling will expresses its choice, says what it would have done, this expression becomes a rule of action for the governed, to be followed until there is a new and different choice

Law.

expressed. This expression of the controlling will is a *law;* and government is control exercised by means of the establishment and enforcement of laws. Thus a father chooses to have his children rise at a certain hour in the morning, and retire at a certain hour in the evening. He tells them plainly what he would have them do; and this expression of his will becomes a law of the family, and remains so, without a new expression, until he chooses to set aside the rule.

Penalty. But the mere expression of the will may not insure control. The child needs to feel that he must obey. This feeling can come only when a penalty is connected with disobedience. This *penalty* consists in the infliction of pain in one form or another. Thus the father says that the child who disobeys the rule shall lose a part of his play-hour. But saying this will do no good, unless the child is sure that the father will do as he says. There must be a certainty that the penalty will be inflicted.

State. The difference between civil government and the others mentioned above is indicated in the meaning of the word "*civil.*" This is derived from the Latin *civilis,* — pertaining to citizens; and a citizen is a member of a state or nation. The following definition of a state is nearly complete: * "A state is a community of persons living within certain limits of territory, under a permanent organization, which aims to secure the prevalence of justice by self-imposed laws." Some would insert after "justice," "and otherwise promote the common weal."

If we examine this definition, we see that the state does not consist of those who directly exercise power, —

* Woolsey's International Law.

not the king, not Congress, not those who vote, — but all the people, a community. The definition excludes wandering tribes of men, and all corporations, which have no limits of territory, and whose object is not justice.

Sovereignty.

If all the laws of the state are self-imposed, that is, if there is no power outside its body of people which dictates to it in any way, the state is said to be *sovereign*. This word does not admit of comparison: one state cannot be more sovereign than another; and a small state, in this respect, stands on an equality with a large one. The sovereignty of a state consists in the absolute right to control its own members, and in the absolute right to resist any interference in its affairs by any other state. The first of these rights constitutes its internal sovereignty; the second, its external sovereignty. From these statements it will be seen that Boston is not a state, that Massachusetts is not a sovereign state. The United States is a sovereign state or nation. Great Britain and Russia are both sovereign states.

Having now defined a state, we are prepared to define civil government as control by law exercised by the state over its members as such.

SUMMARY.

1. Government is control.

2. Intelligence, will, and power are necessary to government.

3. Laws are expressions of the controlling will, which become rules of action for the governed.

4. A law, to secure control, must be accompanied by a penalty, and a certainty that the penalty will be inflicted.

5. A state is a community of persons living within certain limits of territory, under a permanent organization, which aims to secure the prevalence of justice by self-imposed laws.

6. A sovereign state is one in which all the laws are self-imposed.

7. Civil government is control by law, exercised by a state over its members.

CHAPTER II.

SOURCE OF AUTHORITY IN THE STATE.

THE question naturally arises, What right has the state to control me? Why may not I do as I please? To answer this question, we must learn how the state comes to exist.

Necessity of Society.

The members of the state are human beings, and they are, therefore, social beings. They are created with a nature which only the society of fellow-beings can satisfy. They are made to love and hate and fear; and they must have those near them upon whom to exercise these feelings. They have thoughts, and language to express them; and they must be with those who can understand their language, and respond to their thoughts.

If a man lives alone, all these human faculties become dwarfed and stunted for want of exercise; and he is not so much of a man as he might have been. All experience shows that the highest degree of manhood can be attained only in society, and that out of it man grows brutish. A life of solitude, like that of a hermit, always seems unnatural and undesirable. There are stories of human beings who have been exposed in infancy, and have grown up among the brutes; and they are found to have lost the human likeness. They walk upon their hands and feet; their language consists of inarticulate cries and noises; they are afraid of men. Instead of human reason, they have only the instinct of the brute. Centuries ago, Aristotle wrote, "Whoever lives voluntarily out of civil society must have a vicious disposition, or be an existence superior to man." Society, then, is a necessity to man, both for his preservation and for his happiness.

Government a Necessity.

But there are two causes, either of which would make society a failure. Men are selfish, as well as social. Every man has a disposition, more or less strong, to have his own way; and these ways necessarily conflict with each other. If the strongest should succeed, the weak would suffer. Hence quarrels would arise, and society would become a scene of strife and confusion; and the very thing which was designed to preserve human life, and be a means of good to men, would come to be a source of evil.

When men come together in society, they have common wants, which they cannot satisfy as individuals. For instance, the common defence must be provided for; roads and bridges must be built; money must be coined. Men are not only selfish, but they differ in ability to judge wisely; and it would be impossible for all to agree as to the best time and way of doing these things. They would, therefore, remain undone.

To remedy these two evils, society must organize itself permanently, first, to control the evil inclined and protect the weak; and then to devise and carry out plans for the common necessity and convenience. Society so organized is a *state*, and the control which it exercises is *civil government*. The origin of this is evident. It is a necessity of society, and society is a necessity of man's nature.

We are now prepared to answer the question as to the authority of the state. Since civil government is necessary in order that the ends for which society exists may be secured, and since these ends are determined by the nature of man as created, it follows that government comes from God, and that the state derives its authority from him.

Authority from God.

Men in society find themselves under a law of their nature which bids them organize and govern. As in every other case, they are free to obey or disobey, being answerable only to God, who has made the law. But if they disobey they suffer the consequences. They have no security for life and property; virtue and intelligence are wanting; vice and crime prevail: in a word, they are savages; and sooner or later they become the prey of some society which has better fulfilled the end of its creation. All history is full of illustrations of this truth. Our own Indian tribes bear witness that men cannot violate this first duty of society with impunity.

Duty of Society.

Government, therefore, is a *trust* committed to society by the Creator; and society must not only accept the trust, but it is responsible for the way in which it executes it. It is in duty bound to have the best possible government; though what this shall be, it may determine for itself.

Government a Trust.

SUMMARY.

1. Men are social beings; therefore society is a necessity.

2. Men are selfish, and differ in opinion; therefore government is necessary.

3. The state derives its authority from God.

4. Society is under a law requiring it to establish government.

5. Civil government is a trust for which society is responsible to God.

CHAPTER III.

THE GOVERNMENT: ITS FUNCTIONS AND DEPARTMENTS.

In the preceding chapter, we have seen that government is a trust committed to the state. The object of the present chapter is to show by what agencies the state fulfils this trust. In all cases society vests its powers in *a portion of its members.*

The Government.

Those persons, more or less numerous, who directly exercise control over the members of the state, constitute the government thereof. Thus, in the United States, the President and all officers under his control, Congress, and the courts of justice, together form the government.

Distinction between the Government and the State.

It is necessary to fix carefully in the mind the distinction between the state and the government. The former is the whole body of people organized for the purpose of control; the latter is that part of the whole body through which the control is exercised. The state is supreme: the government is subordinate. The right to control rests primarily with the state; secondarily, with the government. All powers belong to the state, being given by the Creator: whatever power the government may have it receives from the state. The government may change: the state remains.

The state is responsible to God; the government, to the state. This is the meaning of the expression in the Declaration of Independence, that governments derive their just powers from the consent of the governed.

Authority how obtained.

As to the way in which they have come to possess these powers, governments may be divided into two classes: first, those to which the people have made formal grants of specified and limited authority; second, those which hold their powers by the tacit consent of the state. It is probable, that, in the early history of the world, all governments were of the latter class. Sometimes a single man, having, in a superior degree, the elements of control, physical strength and skill, courage, and sagacity, came to be recognized by a simple pastoral people as having authority over them. He became their leader in war, and their judge in times of peace. It was likely that his children would share with him the respect and confidence of the people, and in their turn become rulers. Thus, in a simple way, hereditary kingship would come to exist.

In many cases, power has been seized by force, and the people, finding resistance useless, have yielded to the usurpation. Succeeding generations have forgotten that the government was not legitimate, and have suffered its authority to be unquestioned.

There are many states now existing, in which this process has been going on for hundreds and thousands of years; one individual after another assuming control, until the people fail to recognize their own rights and their own responsibility. Such are Russia, Turkey, and the states of Asia. Most of the governments of Europe, and all those of America, are illustrations of the first class.

Since to govern is to control by law, the functions of the government are, to make laws, to interpret and apply them, and to execute them; and these functions call for three departments, —legislative, judicial, and executive.

Functions and Departments.

The relation of these departments to each other may be shown by an illustration. The *legislative* department may make a law saying that no person shall pasture his own cattle on another man's land, and affix a penalty thereto. John Smith is accused of pasturing his horse in his neighbor's field, and thereby violating law. Justice requires, that, if guilty, he shall be punished. The question of his guilt is decided by the *judicial* department. He is brought before a court, where he may deny the act charged, or, admitting it, plead that the word "cattle" in the law does not include horses. In the latter case, the first business of the court is to explain the law. If the decision is that horses are cattle, the act charged being admitted, then the law applies to Smith, and the penalty must be inflicted. A mandate is issued by the court to an *executive* officer, who proceeds to carry out the sentence by imprisoning the man, or by collecting money from him as a fine.

Relation of Departments.

This case may be used to illustrate another most important principle. After the court has decided that the word "cattle" includes horses, it becomes a law that no man shall pasture his *horse* on another's land. If a similar case arises, it is only necessary to refer to this decision; it becomes a precedent for judgment.

Thus it appears that the courts of justice are all the time making law. In fact, much the larger part of all the rules and principles

Laws made by Courts.

that guide the administration of justice in any state is established, not by the legislative department, but by the judiciary.

This difference in origin gives rise to a division of law into two great departments,—statute law, and law that is not statute, included by writers on the subject under the term *unwritten law.*

Statute Law.

Statute law includes all enactments made by legislative bodies, and promulgated by them as laws. These are formed from time to time, as circumstances make them necessary. In process of time some become useless, and are repealed, or changed, or they remain on the statute-book without force. In order to simplify this mass of laws, they are sometimes revised, arranged in a systematic form, and adopted in a body, as comprising all the statute law in force at the time. The so-called Public Statutes of Massachusetts and other States are illustrations of this process.

The Unwritten Law.

The unwritten law consists of all those judicial decisions which have become authoritative through all the periods of the nation's history. This branch of law is a gradual growth, keeping pace with the development of the people's civilization.

As new relations come to exist in society, new cases are constantly coming before the courts for adjustment. In the absence of statutes, the courts must establish principles, which come to have all the force of laws. The chief difference between them and statutes is, that the legislative department may at any time make laws which shall set them aside. Statutes covering the same ground are always superior to the unwritten law.

The term "common law," as used in England and the United States, includes all that portion of the unwritten law of England that has not been set aside by statutes, or by more recent decisions.

Common Law.

SUMMARY.

1. The government of a state consists of those members who directly exercise control within it.

2. The government is subordinate to the state, receiving its authority from it, and being responsible to it.

3. Governments have derived their authority from the state in two ways: first, by formal grants; second, by tacit consent.

4. There are three departments of government: the legislative, which makes the laws; the judicial, which interprets and applies them; the executive, which puts them into operation.

5. Laws are made by the courts of justice, as well as by the legislature.

6. Laws made by the legislature are called statutes; all others are included in the term "the unwritten law."

CHAPTER IV.

FORMS OF GOVERNMENTS, AND MEANS BY WHICH THEY ARE LIMITED.

THE following forms of governments have been described by writers upon the subject: —

Absolute Monarchy. An Absolute Monarchy is a government in which the laws are made by one person, and interpreted and executed by officers responsible only to him. Examples: Russia, Turkey, Persia.

Limited Monarchy. A Limited Monarchy is a government in which there is an hereditary executive, and a legislative department whose members are chosen periodically by the people, the judiciary being responsible directly to the sovereign. Examples: England, Sweden and Norway, Denmark. Rarely, in such governments, the sovereign is elected.

Republic. A Representative Democracy, or Republic, is a government in which both the chief executive and the members of the legislative department are chosen periodically by the people. The judiciary may be appointed by the executive, or be elected by the people. Examples: United States, Mexico, States of Central America.

Democracy. A government in which the whole body of people meet to make the laws is sometimes called a Pure Democracy. This is possible only in a small state. The government of some of the early English colonies in America was of this sort.

Other Forms.

There have been states in which all the functions of government were in the hands of a few people, self-appointed. Such a government is an Oligarchy. If a class of nobles rules the state, the government is called an Aristocracy.

Some governments combine several different features. Thus, in the government of England, the executive department represents the monarchy. The legislative department consists of two bodies, one aristocratic, the other republican. In most states, the legislature consists of two bodies ; in others, of one.

Absolute Governments.

These various forms may be divided into two classes, —absolute, and limited. In a certain sense, no government now existing is really absolute. In all so called absolute governments there are immemorial customs which restrict the sovereign in the exercise of power, and each ruler follows in the steps of his predecessor. If his people are at all intelligent, he will not dare to make radical changes. But there is no way to call him to account except by rebellion, and history shows that nations will submit to oppression for a long period rather than take up arms against the established government.

An absolute government may furnish civil liberty to its subjects, and may do much to promote their happiness ; but, at any time, a different man may come into power, and anarchy or oppression ensue. There is no security beyond the present. For this reason, such a government cannot be, in the highest sense, a good one, though it may be the best possible under the circumstances: indeed, it may be the only form possible over a rude, lawless people.

Constitutions.

Since the possession of power creates a desire for more, the tendency of all governments is away from the people. It becomes necessary for a state which values its welfare, to impose some restraints upon its government. It must express its will definitely, and hold the government answerable as subject to law. This law by which the state controls the government is its constitution. It usually specifies the rights of the people, which the government is to respect; states how the departments shall be constituted, thus fixing the form of the government; enumerates in detail the functions of each; provides a mode of calling the government to account, and of making needed changes; prescribes the manner in which the will of the state shall be expressed; and makes provision for changing the constitution itself.

Thus the constitution of the United States asserts the rights of the people; says that there shall be a President, a Congress of two houses, and certain courts of justice; gives to the President power to pardon, to act as commander-in-chief of the army and navy, and to execute the laws; gives Congress powers over finance, territory, and commerce; fixes the term of office of all members of the government; states who shall vote, and how the constitution may be amended.

It will be seen that the constitution becomes the fundamental law of a state, and that all others must accord with it. If they do not, they are void. This question of constitutionality of laws is usually decided by the judicial department, never by the citizen.

Written Constitutions.

Constitutions are of two kinds. Some are written instruments drawn up and adopted at one time, either by the people for themselves when establishing a new form of government, as in the United States; or by the existing government, as in the case of Austria, which, after the exercise of arbitrary power, wished to conciliate the discontented people of Hungary.

Unwritten Constitutions.

Others are unwritten, having no distinct, definite form, but consisting of all legislative acts, royal grants, and judicial decisions, by which at any time the form of the government has been established, and by which the rights of the people are guaranteed, and the powers of the government restricted. Such is the British constitution, which has been growing into its present form for a thousand years. It bears the marks of all the social and political changes which have succeeded each other during the rule of Saxon, Norman, and English sovereigns. In another place the development of this constitution will be noticed.

The unwritten constitution is open to the objection that it may be changed by the government itself, and thus cease to express the people's will. Thus a certain parliament changed its term of office from three to seven years, thereby prolonging its power, and preventing a new expression of the people's will. In the United States, with its written constitution, such a change could only be made by the people.

Checks upon the Government.

How shall the government be made to obey the constitution, so that it may be effective to prevent arbitrary rule? This is done in two ways. Usually, the departments are so constituted that each acts as a check upon the other. Thus in the United States, the President must approve all bills passed by a majority in Congress, before they can become laws. The Senate must consent to all treaties, and to all important appointments made by the President. Without such consent they are not valid. The judges are appointed by the President and Senate, and they decide upon the constitutionality of laws made by Congress. If either branch of the government attempts to violate the constitution, the others may in this way prevent it.

Limitation of Term.

But the most effective way of preventing the exercise of unconstitutional authority is by limiting the term of office of the members of the government. At the expiration of a specified time, the office becomes vacant, and the people are called upon to re-fill it. They may re-appoint the former incumbent. This is a verdict of approval of his administration. If they select a new man, the act may imply dissatisfaction. When the people have this power of changing the government at their will, it becomes impossible for any usurpation of authority to continue. It is only when men may be re-elected to the same office that this limitation of term becomes a salutary check. If they must give up the position, whether faithful or not, the temptation is strong to use it for selfish ends. The election ceases to be a popular judgment upon the character of the administration. For this reason, the principle of rotation in office is one of the most mischievous that can guide the action of an intelligent people.

Expression of Popular Will.

We have described a constitution as a formal expression of the will of the state, granting authority to the government; and we have also said that under limited governments the state is frequently called upon to pass judgment upon the administration. It is important to show how the state expresses its will. What is the voice of the people?

The whole body of people comprising the state includes some who are not capable of judging wisely concerning the general good; to this class evidently belong children and imbeciles. Every state is therefore divided into two classes,—those who have a voice in public affairs, and those who have not; the voting, and the non-voting. The line of division varies greatly in different states. In most women are included in the latter class. Sometimes color is made a ground of disqualification for voting, sometimes poverty, sometimes a certain form of religious belief, sometimes the inability to read and write. In all cases those who *do* vote decide who *may* vote. In every state, for the non-voting class the government is absolute; they are responsible for it only on the ground of tacit consent. Those who have a voice in the conduct of public affairs are said to have political liberty.

Voters and Non-Voters.

Voting is expressing a choice; and it seldom happens that a large number of people are unanimous in their opinions. In case of disagreement, either the few or the many must give up to the others, or there will be no decision. Justice requires that the will of the smaller number shall submit to that of the larger. Hence the common rule that the majority decides.

Majority Rule.

It appears, therefore, that, when we speak of an election as expressing the will of the state, we mean that it is the choice of more than half of the voting population, submitted to by all the others. This supposes that all persons vote who can do so, which is far from being the case. Thus in one State the returns of one election were as follows:—

Population	1,651,652
Voting class	351,056
Votes for successful candidate for governor	83,639

It appears that only one in twenty of the members of the State actually expressed a preference for the governor chosen in that year. In other years a larger proportion of the voters had voted, but seldom more than one in eight of the members of the State. Many schemes have been devised by which the minority may also be represented, but none have come into general use.

SUMMARY.

1. The forms of government that have existed are, absolute monarchy, limited monarchy, republic, democracy, aristocracy, oligarchy.
2. Absolute governments are restricted by custom, but cannot be called to account except by rebellion.
3. A constitution is a law by which the state controls the government.
4. The constitution is the fundamental law, and all others must accord with it.
5. Some constitutions are written instruments; others are without definite form.
6. The departments of a government should be able to check one another.
7. The authority of government is limited by limiting the term of service of its members.
8. The whole body of people in the state is divided into voters and non-voters.
9. The voice of a majority of those who vote is considered to express the will of the state.
10. This is usually a very small part of the whole body.

CHAPTER V.

OBLIGATIONS OF THE GOVERNMENT.

WE have seen that the people commit to a part of their number their authority, to be used for the common good. We have now to examine this trust in detail, and ascertain what a government should do to be a good one.

Its several obligations may be classified in three divisions: first, to secure justice to the members of the state; second, to promote the general welfare; third, to defend the state.

Three Duties.

In order to secure justice, it is the duty of the government to protect every individual, without distinction, in the enjoyment of his natural rights. These rights are included under four heads, — the right of personal security, the right of personal liberty, the right of private property, and the right of religious belief and worship.

Justice, how secured.

The Right of Personal Security is the right to enjoy life, body, health, and reputation. It means not merely the right to live, but to live in safety and tranquillity, without fear and without the necessity for self-defence. No greater reproach can be brought against a state than to say that human life is not secure within its territory. When deeds of vio-

Personal Security.

lence and blood are frequent and unpunished, the government fails to meet its first great duty.

Modes of Making Life Secure. Life is rendered more secure by making murder the highest crime known to the law, and punishable by death. If the penalty for homicide were no greater than for theft, murder would be much more frequent than now. The government shows its regard for the safety of human life and limb by the care with which it investigates all cases of loss of life from doubtful causes. **Inquests.** If a human body is found under circumstances which make it probable that a crime has been committed, an officer, under the authority of the government, at once proceeds to an inquiry, to learn the cause of death, that the guilty party, if there be such, may be brought to justice. If a railroad accident has occasioned loss of life, an inquest is held to ascertain the cause of the disaster, and to fix the responsibility, so that justice may be done.

Security of Travellers. The government also compels corporations to take precautions for the safety of their own employees, and of the public whom they serve. Thus railway companies are obliged to have bells on locomotives, and to have them rung at highway crossings, to place signs over such crossings, and to station flagmen at some of them, to stop their trains before crossing another railroad, to provide a certain number of brakemen for each passenger train. Owners of steamboats are required to equip them with boats, buckets, life-preservers, and all appliances by which the safety of passengers may be promoted.

The government maintains buoys and lighthouses, and removes obstructions from harbors and rivers for the safety of mariners. It prohibits fast driving in public streets, and stations officers to assist foot-passengers over crossings. All these provisions have the same general end.

Nor is a good government any less mindful of the health of the people. It takes precautions to prevent the spread of contagious diseases. It appoints officers whose business it is to require cleanliness in cities; and it may cause filthy, overcrowded, or unsafe houses to be vacated. It restricts the sale of poisons, prohibits the sale of unwholesome food, and requires certain kinds of business — as powder-making and bone-boiling — to be carried on at a distance from habitations. It supports hospitals and asylums for the comfort and recovery of the sick.

Modes of Securing Health.

Next to life, honest men value reputation. Every person has a right to be thought as well of as his character will allow. Therefore he may demand protection against all false and malicious utterances which tend to destroy his peace or to injure his business. Such utterances, if spoken, constitute slander, and, if written or printed, libel; and both should be punished by the government.

Reputation.

The Right of Personal Liberty is, primarily, the right to go and come without restraint; but its meaning has been extended to cover freedom of speech and of the press, the right to assemble peaceably for discussion, the right to petition the government, and freedom from unreasonable search of property and papers. It is only within two hundred years that these last have been considered natural rights, and still in many states they are not allowed.

Personal Liberty.

Habeas Corpus.

The most important means by which personal liberty is directly secured to the subject is the writ of *habeas corpus.* This is a written instrument issued by a judge or court, directed to a person holding another in custody, commanding him to bring the prisoner before the judge or court at a certain time and place, to show why he holds him. How this operates may be shown by illustrations. A minor enlisted in the United States army without the consent of his parents or guardian, an act which was contrary to law. A judge issued a writ of habeas corpus to the commanding officer, who, in obedience to the summons, brought the boy before the court, and stated the manner of enlistment. The judge discharged the boy. A girl about fourteen years of age had been bound to service in Canada. The man whom she served went with her to Massachusetts, where her mother obtained a writ of habeas corpus to recover the child. The man appeared before the court with the child, where it was made apparent that she was well treated, and that she preferred to remain with her master. The court refused to give her to the mother. In Boston the sheriff had arrested and imprisoned a man in consequence of a suit concerning a partnership in which he was interested. His friends procured a writ of habeas corpus; being brought before the court, and his case heard, he was discharged, on the ground that the circumstances were such that imprisonment was illegal.

Since the officers of the law may thus arrest and detain persons without sufficient cause, and so the government itself infringe upon the liberty of its subjects, the privilege of demanding this writ is considered one of the strongest safeguards that a people can have. More than any other one thing this marks the distinction between a free government and a despotism, and to withdraw it is always perilous to the liberties of the people.

Right of Private Property.

The Right of Private Property covers the acquiring, using, and disposing of any thing that a person may call his own, including time and labor. This right may be violated in so many ways that the government has more call to exercise its control in this direction than in all others combined. A man's property may be stolen, or burned, or damaged, or taken from him on false pretences, or borrowed and not returned. His wages, or his interest, or his rents, may not be paid; and, if he succeed in holding his own while he lives, at his death it may be scattered beyond his control. Against all these evils it is the duty of the government to protect every member of the state. It must guard his right to labor, against all who from any motive would hinder him; and it must carry out his will as to the disposition of his property after his death. That this general right may be secured, laws are made respecting theft, arson, and fraud; concerning corporations, and the relations of debtor and creditor, master and servant, landlord and tenant; laws regulating tenures, deeds and wills; usury and trespass laws; and laws respecting stocks, bonds, and notes.

Religious Liberty.

Religious liberty, as understood by the people of the United States, is the right of every individual to hold such form of religious belief as he chooses, or to have none at all, and to worship as he pleases, or not at all. The government is bound to treat all forms of belief alike, and to protect each person in his own. Practically, by Sunday laws and official and judicial oaths, the governments of most of the States of the Union recognize Christianity; but there is no restriction of civil or political rights because of any form of belief or unbelief.

Natural Liberty.

In describing rights as natural, it is meant that they are necessary to the fullest development of the individual. His human nature demands them; and, when free to do so, he instinctively exercises them. The freedom to do so without any restraint is sometimes described as natural liberty. This is supposed to represent the condition of men without society, each person gratifying his inclinations to the fullest extent.

Natural Rights Limited.

But, since every man is born into society, he is hedged about on all sides by limitations to these natural rights. Natural liberty is only an idea. A man may do as he pleases in any direction, only as far as he does not interfere with the right of another man in the same direction. Each separate right that has been spoken of is limited at just this point. I have a right to walk; but I may not walk over my neighbor's field nor through his house without leave. I have a right to acquire, use, and dispose of property and time; but I cannot get money by fraud, nor keep what I find, nor burn my house, nor spend my time in idleness as a vagabond. I have a right to speak freely upon any subject I choose; but I cannot utter slander with impunity. I have a right to worship God without restraint according to the dictates of my own conscience; but I may not practise a religion whose rights are obscene or cruel.

These natural rights are also limited in another direction. While it is the duty of the government to protect the individual in the enjoyment of his property, it may compel him to give up a portion of it for the public good. This right of the government, thus limiting that of the subject, exists in two forms: first, as the right of *taxation;* second, as the right of *eminent domain.* The first is based on the facts, that the administration of government is for the general good, and that whatever benefits the whole benefits each member of society. Hence the government may require each to bear his proportionate share of the public expense. If he refuses to do this, his property may be sold for the purpose.

Right of Taxation.

Upon this subject Chief Justice Marshall says, "The power of taxing the people and their property is essential to the very existence of government, and may be legitimately exercised on the objects to which it is applicable, to the utmost extent to which the government may choose to carry it."

The Right of Eminent Domain allows the government to take the private property of an individual, and use it for the public good. Thus, if a schoolhouse is to be built, the government may choose a site, and then compel the owner to give up the land for the purpose. This right differs from that of taxation in that it is exercised upon some individuals, and not upon all; and also in that compensation is rendered for the property taken, the price being fixed by disinterested persons chosen for the purpose. The government frequently exercises this right through corporations. Thus railway companies are allowed to take the land they need along a specified route.

Right of Eminent Domain.

It thus appears that personal rights are limited in

two directions,—first, by the rights of one's neighbors; second, by the necessities of the state itself. The free enjoyment of one's natural rights, subject to these two limitations, constitutes civil liberty. It is liberty under law; and we are prepared to state, as the first requisite of a good government, that it shall furnish this to every member of the state.

Civil Liberty.

But these rights are not only limited: they may be forfeited. When a man, in the exercise of his freedom, has violated the right of another, he has become an enemy to the state; and government, to protect society, may take away his personal liberty by imprisonment, or his property by fine, or even his life.

Forfeiture of Rights.

SUMMARY.

1. The duties of the government are, to secure justice, to promote the general welfare, to defend the state.

2. Justice is secured by protecting every individual in his right to personal security, personal liberty, private property, and his own religious belief and worship.

3. It is the duty of government to care for the life, health, and reputation of its subjects.

4. Personal liberty is freedom to go and come, to assemble peaceably for discussion, to petition the government, and freedom of speech and of the press.

5. Personal liberty is secured by means of the writ of habeas corpus.

6. The right of private property covers the acquiring, using, and disposing of property, time, and labor.

7. These are called natural rights because every man instinctively exercises them.

8. They are limited in society, first, by a regard to the right of others; second, by the right of the government to take property for public purposes.

9. This right of the government exists as the right of taxation, and the right of eminent domain.

10. Civil liberty is the enjoyment of one's natural rights in society. It is liberty under law.

11. These rights may be forfeited by the commission of crime.

CHAPTER VI.

OBLIGATIONS OF THE GOVERNMENT (CONTINUED).

Promotion of General Welfare.

IN securing justice, the government is taking the best possible means to promote the public happiness and improvement. Civil liberty is the ground of national prosperity. In states where anarchy and misrule have long prevailed, the people are poor, and the country is unproductive.

Measures of Public Utility.

Yet there are means by which the government may act more directly to this end. Among these are, educating the people, and carrying out measures of public utility and convenience. The most obvious of these are the establishment of means of communication, as roads and bridges, postal arrangements, and the coining of money. In all these, that uniformity which is so necessary can only be secured by having the government assume the control.

Fostering Industries.

The government can do much to foster the industries of the nation. Thus the United States, in the interest of commerce, surveys its coast, provides maps and charts, clears its rivers and harbors, builds breakwaters, enacts pilotage laws, prepares and publishes weather reports, and sends its officers and ships of war to foreign ports to protect its seamen. It promotes agriculture by maintaining experiment stations to test whether the productions of other countries might not be raised in the United States, by collecting and scattering new seeds and plants, and by disseminating information of new and improved modes of carrying on the business. It has given bounties to persons engaged in certain kinds of fishing. It aims to encourage manufactures by placing duties upon foreign goods, so that home productions may have an advantage in the market. It has given lands and money to aid in building railroads and canals, and in establishing steamship lines to foreign ports. It maintains a bureau of forestry to gather and disseminate information as to the best management, use, and preservation of woodlands, so that lumbering may be continued without the destruction of the forests.

Education.

The duty of the government to provide for the education of the people rests upon the same basis as its obligations to care for the public health and public morals. Ignorance is so fruitful a source of poverty and crime, that the government is striking at the root of many evils when it labors to promote the general intelligence of the community. It is bound, therefore, to provide the rudiments of an education for all the children under its authority. Beyond this the best governments furnish opportunities to all who desire a higher culture, not only intellectual, but in professional and industrial pursuits.

If the government is bound to furnish schools for its youth, it is also bound to compel their attendance. It should not allow the carelessness or avarice of parents to deprive their children of what is so essential to their welfare and happiness.

Public Education in Republics.

There are other and stronger reasons why a democratic republic should encourage popular education. All the interests of the state are directly in the hands of the mass of the people. The officers are chosen by the people and from the people. What the voters are, the government will be. The ignorance and vice that prevail among the people will be represented in the government, as surely as the intelligence and the virtue. A corrupt public sentiment produces corrupt legislation and corrupt administration; and these produce weakness and decay. Hence the interests of every citizen are, in a measure, in the hands of every other citizen; and to protect himself he must use all his influence to make his neighbor as intelligent and virtuous as himself. The education needs to be not only intellectual, but moral and religious. All that the statutes of Massachusetts require is needed in every republic. That state makes it the duty of all instructors of youth, to exert their best endeavors to impress upon the minds of their pupils "the principles of piety and justice, and a sacred regard for truth; love of their country, humanity, and universal benevolence; sobriety, industry, and frugality; chastity, moderation, and temperance; and those other virtues which are the ornament of human society, and the basis upon which a republican constitution is founded."

General Culture.

There are some educating influences besides schools. Public libraries, museums, and galleries of art do much to promote the general intelligence, and to refine and cultivate the taste. Public parks and gardens furnish means of healthful and innocent enjoyment. It may seem that these are outside the province of government, and that it should not tax the people for such purposes. But experience has shown that cultivated minds and hearts, and refined tastes, result in softened manners; that educated people understand better their relations and obligations in society, and have more respect for law and order, than the ignorant; and that from the lowest motive, economy, it is better to prevent crime than to punish it.

Defence of the State.

The third comprehensive duty of the government is to defend the state against foreign and domestic enemies. In doing this, it is to be prompt and vigorous; and it may make use of all the resources of the state. There can be no limitations upon its authority in this direction. The existence of the state is so important that all ordinary considerations of economy become insignificant. The government may draw upon the wealth of the people to exhaustion; and it may demand their personal services and their lives, until resistance becomes useless. It may suspend all its ordinary operations in an extremity. But all this sacrifice of money and of human life and happiness is for defence, not for aggression. The government has no right to involve the state in war simply to increase its territory, or to extend its power.

International Relations.

For, intimately connected with its duty to protect the state, is its obligation to other states. It is bound to respect their right to exist, and to refrain from acts of injustice and oppression. It must recognize their sovereignty, and treat them with proper courtesy. It must respect the person and property of every member of every other state, and it must do all in its power to promote mutual good feeling among all the nations.

International Law. These are called international obligations, and when formally stated constitute what is called International Law. Thus, when Great Britain allowed the piratical "Alabama" to sail from her ports to destroy the commerce of the United States, she was said to violate the law of nations. When Russia, Prussia, and Austria divided Poland among themselves, they committed the highest crime possible against a sovereign state. When the Boxers attacked the foreigners residing in China and destroyed their property, the Chinese government was responsible for the violation of international rights.

International Law Peculiar. The law of nations differs from all other law in that it is not the expression of a controlling will. There is no human authority above that of a sovereign state; so that this law is only a collection of rules which nations acknowledge as binding upon them in their relations with each other. This law is also peculiar in that there is no umpire to settle disputes, and no penalty. If a state violates the law of nations, the injured party can only obtain redress by war, unless the guilty state chooses to make amends in some other way. Thus, in the case of China, the Allied Powers have by force compelled the payment of a large indemnity. The "Alabama" case was submitted to a board of arbitration, which decided that Great Britain should pay a certain sum for property destroyed through her negligence. There is now a permanent Court of Arbitration, having its seat at The Hague, the capital of Holland, to which nations may submit their disputes. The court consists of distinguished jurists chosen by the leading nations of the world. It is hoped that this court may promote the peace of the world.

SUMMARY.

1. By securing justice, the government promotes the general welfare.

2. It does this also by executing measures of public utility, and by fostering the industries of the state.

3. It is the duty of the government to provide for the education of the people.

4. The government may compel children to attend school.

5. The government should care for the general culture of the people.

6. It is a duty of the government to defend the state. To do this it may draw without limit upon the wealth and the services of the people.

7. The government is bound to respect the rights of other states.

8. Certain rules are recognized by nations as guiding them in their intercourse with each other. These constitute International Law.

9. Until recently there has been no mode of effecting a final settlement of international disputes but by force. Within a few years resort has been had to arbitration. There is now a permanent international Court of Arbitration.

CHAPTER VII.

NATURE AND DUTIES OF CITIZENSHIP.

THE state has been defined as a community of people.

Citizens and Aliens.

A citizen of a state is a member of this community, who is entitled to be protected by the government in the enjoyment of his civil rights, both at home and abroad. A person residing within a country, but not a citizen, is an alien.

Classes of Citizens.

There are two classes of citizens, — native and naturalized. Native citizens are those members of the state who were born within its territory, or whose parents were natives. Naturalized citizens were once aliens, but have become citizens by complying with certain legal requirements. The second class have all the civil rights and duties of the first, but certain political privileges are sometimes withheld. Thus none but native citizens can hold the office of President or Vice-President of the United States.

Duty of Support.

Citizenship, like all other relations, has certain duties peculiar to itself. The individual who enjoys the protection of the government is bound to support it. He may do this in part by respecting its authority, and by obeying its laws. A government is strong in proportion as it can command the obedience of its subjects. Evasion of law is as bad as wilful violation of it; inasmuch as it shows a want of respect, which needs only to have the fear of punishment removed to become disobedience. Every good citizen holds the spirit of a law as sacred as the letter. One who breaks any law of the state violates the right of those for whose protection the law was made.

Obedience.

This duty of obedience is limited in one direction. When to obey a law of the state would be to disobey a clearly revealed law of God, the obligation to God takes precedence, and the citizen is bound to disobey. This is a question of conscience, and as such must be decided by each individual for himself. But the government may not recognize this as a valid excuse for disobedience. If it did so, the most unscrupulous would become the most conscientious. It must treat disobedience as such, and punish it accordingly. Nor has a citizen any ground of complaint. If his respect for the divine government is so great, he must also respect the government of the state enough to suffer the consequences of his scruples willingly.

Conscientious Disobedience.

Besides the moral support which comes from respect and obedience, the citizen is bound to contribute of his means to meet the necessary expenses of the government. These expenses are incurred for the benefit of all. Every citizen enjoys personal security and personal liberty; and, if he has property, that is also protected. For all this, justice requires that he shall pay in proportion to his means. This obligation is as binding as any between man and

Pecuniary Support.

man; and wilful evasion of it is as dishonorable as any other form of fraud.

Defence.

The citizen is also bound to support the government by force of arms. The benefits of government are so many that no sacrifice can be considered too great that its safety makes necessary. The highest virtue of a citizen utters itself in the saying, "It is sweet to die for one's country."

Patriotism.

A citizen who meets these obligations cheerfully is a patriot. To obey the laws because they are laws, to pay one's taxes without grumbling, to give up friends or one's own life, if necessary — these are the evidences of patriotism.

Duty to Vote.

Another weighty obligation rests upon the subjects of a limited government. They are bound to *vote*.

The Right of Suffrage.

Voting, or suffrage as it is called, is often spoken of as a right. There is an historical reason for this. All the limited governments of the present day have grown out of more absolute ones. In every state there has been a time when the government was supposed to derive its authority directly from God, not from the people. They had no voice in establishing the government, nor in administering it. From various causes, in different countries, the existing government, usually a sovereign, either alone or with an aristocracy, gave to a portion of the people suffrage as a privilege. These extended it to others, until the voting class in each state has come to be what it is. When people have once enjoyed the privilege of voting, they have claimed it as a right, basing the claim upon the fact that it has been given by the government. For the last century the tendency has been toward universal suffrage.

Whatever opinion may be held as to the limits placed upon suffrage, there can be no doubt that whoever may vote ought to vote. **Basis of Obligation to Vote.** The obligation upon the state to have the best government rests upon every individual to the extent of his possible influence. If he have a voice in the selection of officers, and so in making the laws, he is as much bound to use his opportunity for good as to perform the commonest act of honesty or charity. The difference is so wide between a good government and a bad one, the interests at stake are so precious, that indifference in politics becomes a crime. Voting is a *trust* held by the few for the interest of the many: to use it, and to use it conscientiously, this is to promote order and happiness; and not to use it, or to abuse it, is to take the part of those who prey upon society for their personal profit.

The duty to have a good government rests upon the subjects of absolute authority, as well as upon those who have a vote in controlling the state. **Duty of Revolution.** When the government fails to meet its obligations to the people, when its acts are injurious rather than beneficial, the people are bound to seek a change either in the form of the government, or in the mode of its administration. This is the duty of revolution. This change may be effected in either of two ways: first, by what is termed moral resistance, that is, by complaint, petition, and refusing to aid in enforcing the law; or, second, when there is just ground of complaint, when the other method has failed, and there is a fair prospect of success, by armed opposition.

The third condition deserves notice as illustrating a general principle. Though the acts of a government may be ever so oppressive, it is better to suffer them for a time, than to start a rebellion which cannot succeed. The evils resulting to the state from a civil war are so enormous, that to begin such a contest for trivial reasons, or against overwhelming odds, is the highest crime that can be committed against the welfare of society. The frequent revolutions which have characterized the republics of South and Central America have retarded their progress and weakened their influence.

Government bound to punish Rebellion.

The duty of the government here is as plain as that of the individual. While one may be bound to rebel, the other is as much bound to resist. The man who undertakes to overthrow the established government takes his life in his hands. The government must regard rebels as traitors, and if they are unsuccessful must punish them as such. If the cause is a worthy one, rebels may be patriots; and, if successful, their names may go down to posterity with honor. The British government looked upon Washington as a rebel and a criminal; America considers him a model of political virtue.

Nature of Political Duties.

The various duties of the citizen, that have been enumerated, are moral obligations with all the weight of such. They are things to do or not to do, to do well or ill, demanding choice, and involving responsibility. They go along with such obligations as honesty, chastity, and temperance, and come under the great law of human relation which requires every man to love his neighbor as himself.

SUMMARY.

1. A citizen is a member of the state.
2. A citizen may be native or naturalized.

3. Persons on being naturalized usually have all the civil rights and duties of native-born citizens.

4. Every citizen is bound to support the government by obeying its laws.

5. He is bound to disobey a law which violates his conscience; but he must suffer the penalties of disobedience.

6. Every citizen is bound to support the government with his money, and by his service if necessary to its defence.

7. Voting is a duty.

8. Suffrage is called a right because it has been conferred as such gradually by absolute governments.

9. Revolution may be a duty. Armed revolution is justifiable only as a last resort, and when success is probable.

10. The government should punish rebels.

11. Political duties are moral obligations.

PART II.

CIVIL GOVERNMENT IN THE STATES BEFORE THEIR INDEPENDENCE.

CHAPTER VIII.

ESTABLISHMENT OF CIVIL, RELIGIOUS, AND POLITICAL LIBERTY IN ENGLAND.

As most of the settlers of the thirteen colonies were from England, it is necessary to know what notions of government they brought with them; and to do this we must trace the development of civil institutions in the mother country. We shall find that nearly all that is best in our government had been secured by centuries of conflict in Great Britain.

Under the Anglo-Saxon kings,[1] people were divided into two great classes, — freemen and slaves. Two classes of freemen existed, — those who owned land, and those who did not.

County Courts.

The country was divided into Counties, in each of which a Court was held periodically, presided over by an alderman. This court was an assembly of freemen; and it is doubtful if any but land-owners voted. Before this body, wills and deeds were attested; and it was also a court of justice. At first the whole body of people decided matters in dispute. Afterward, in each case, a body of men, usually twelve, acquainted with the facts, gave a decision upon oath. This was the germ of the modern jury system.

[1] See close of chapter for list of sovereigns of England.

The system was gradually developed by employing men not acquainted with the facts, and bringing witnesses before them to testify; and a further change was made when the decision of questions of law was given to a judge, leaving to the jury only questions of fact. The county officers were elected by the freemen at these courts.

The King.

The central government was vested in a king, who came to the throne by hereditary title, but also, usually, with the consent of the larger land-owners. Associated with him in the management of affairs was a body called the Assembly of the Wise Men. Originally all the land-owners were entitled to a seat in this assembly; but after a time only the more powerful exercised the right. This body had power to raise troops for national defence, to impose taxes, to direct ecclesiastical affairs, and to care for the general interests of the state. The body met only when convoked by the king.

The Great Council.

Thus it appears, that the government was a limited monarchy, that the great body of the people had no voice in its administration, that the local institutions afforded considerable liberty to the lower classes of freemen, and were designed to secure justice to all.

The Feudal System.

The Norman Conquest (1066) wrought some most important changes. The Feudal System was introduced. By this the king was considered the proprietor of all lands, and distributed them among the people as he chose. To some he gave lands for which they were to pay a fixed rent; but most held estates on condition of rendering a stipulated amount of military service. The holders were called the king's vassals, and held the property for a specified time, or for life; and later the title became hereditary. As king's vassals they were entitled to a seat in his council. These men granted portions of their estates to subordinates on similar terms.

Feudal Abuses.

Many abuses crept into the system. Besides the military service, the king's vassals were required to furnish money to ransom the king's person, and on the marriage of his eldest daughter. If a vassal died, the king received money of the heir on coming to the property: if the heir was not of age, the king became his guardian, and received the revenues of the estate. Often, in place of the military service, the kings demanded money.

Two Councils.

Besides the great council composed of the king's vassals, there came to be a smaller one consisting of those officers of state who were immediately attached to the king's person. This latter body came to exercise all the administrative part of the government under the authority of the king. The king interfered in the local administration by withdrawing an important part of the business from the county courts, and giving it to justices of his own appointment. Some of the county officers also came to be appointed by the king.

Norman Oppression.

In all these ways the Norman sovereigns oppressed their subjects; and person and property were not secure from their arbitrary rule. During all this time the barons struggled against the unjust exactions; and each king, on coming to the throne, granted a charter in which he solemnly promised to respect the ancient laws, and to refrain from oppressive acts. But these promises were never kept.

Magna Charta.

During the reign of John, who was both weak and mean, the barons, under arms, compelled him to sign the famous instrument called Magna Charta (1215). The larger part of this consisted of concessions to the barons, remedying feudal abuses. It also established a fixed mode of administering justice, setting up in the counties a court to be held by two judges appointed by the king, and four knights chosen by the county. The most important declaration was as follows:—

"No freeman shall be arrested, or imprisoned, or dispossessed of his tenement, or outlawed, or exiled, or in any wise proceeded against; we will not place or cause to be placed hands upon him, unless by the legal judgment of his peers, or by the law of the land. Justice shall not be sold, refused, or delayed to any one." It will be seen that here was a promise of complete civil liberty to every freeman. But John and the kings who succeeded him evaded these charters in every possible way, and, though repeatedly taking oath to respect them, were always violating them.

Origin of the House of Commons.

It had always been a fundamental principle, that the king could lay no taxes without the consent of his council, though every king had done so. In the early part of the thirteenth century, the lesser vassals of the king, though not attending the council, had considerable prominence in the counties; and associated with them was an important class of land-owners who held their property on other than feudal terms. These were the so-called English yeomanry. The kings, hoping to secure a party in the council in their interest, began the practice of summoning a certain number of men from the counties, to be chosen by those smaller land-owners as their representatives. These men were called knights of the shire. About the same time, many towns had acquired wealth and importance; and to secure their influence, and also that they might be taxed with their own consent, they were invited to send deputies to the assembly (1250–1300). These were called borough members. There was no system in the matter. Those boroughs which were called upon were represented, and only those. The right came to be based upon custom, so that in process of time many large towns grew up without representation, while old but decayed boroughs retained the ancient privilege. This was the cause of the evil of "rotten boroughs," which created so much agitation in the early part of the present century.

Parliament.

Thus it appears that during the thirteenth century the limiting body came to consist of three parts, — first, the barons and bishops, sitting by their own right; second, the knights of the shire, elected by the land-owners of the counties; third, the borough members, elected by those who managed the local affairs in the towns. The last two classes, having interests in common, after a time united, and formed the House of Commons; the other constituted the House of Lords: the whole made up the Parliament.

Power of the Commons.

At first the Commons had little share in the government except to assent to taxation. If they had grievances to be redressed, or new measures to propose, they framed petitions, and presented them to the king through their presiding officer, for this reason called Speaker. These requests were so frequently disregarded, that they gradually adopted the surer method of framing their wishes into statutes, and then presenting them to the king for his approval. They claimed the right of free discussion, and then the right to examine into public expenditures, and to hold the king's ministers responsible for maladministration. All these were signs that the idea of the government's responsibility to the state was gaining ground.

Arbitrary Rule of the Tudors.

On the accession of the Tudors (1485), they found the nobility greatly weakened by the long civil wars that had preceded, and the commons had not yet acquired the courage to defend their rights stoutly. The result was, that under Henry VII. and Henry VIII. the people suffered the most gross and oppressive exactions. When Parliament objected to voting money, the king's ministers raised it by illegal modes of taxation. One of these ministers told the merchants whom he was trying to fleece, that those who lived expensively thus showed their wealth, and those who lived prudently must have grown rich by economy, and so both classes could afford to be taxed.

Personal security was no more inviolate than property. Hallam says, "A single suspicion in the dark bosom of Henry VII., a single cloud of wayward humor in his son, would have been sufficient to send the proudest peer of England to the dungeon and the scaffold." During the reign of these two men, the authority of the king was more nearly absolute than at any other period of English history. The complete establishment of civil and political liberty came after a century and a half of agitation respecting religion.

Power of the Church.

The Roman Catholic was the only religion in England and on the Continent. Immense estates were connected with the churches and monasteries, and the wealthy bishops and abbots had seats in Parliament, and great influence in the state. The pope as supreme head of the church claimed also the right to interfere in some of the civil affairs of the nations; but the English people had always been jealous of this interference, though not always able to resist successfully.

The Separation from Rome.

Henry VIII., having quarrelled with the pope about a divorce, renounced his allegiance, and was proclaimed by Parliament supreme head of the church in England (1534). By this act the English Catholic Church became a separate body; and after this time the king and Parliament had complete control of the appointment of church officers, and the regulation of church affairs. Henry abolished the monasteries, and confiscated their property to the crown.

The Protestant Reformation.

During this reign the Protestant Reformation began in Germany under Luther (1517); and the doctrines of the new religion spread rapidly over Europe and in England. Henry VIII., though he quarrelled with the pope, was still a Catholic. He persecuted the Protestants for heresy, while he also punished the Catholics who refused to acknowledge his supremacy.

The Reformation in England.

Edward VI., though a boy when he became king (1547), had decided opinions in favor of the Protestants; and the chief of his advisers sympathized with him. They at once began the work of change. The church services, which had always been in Latin, were changed by the preparation of a prayer-book in English which omitted the leading Catholic doctrines. Images were removed from the churches, and many of the ceremonies of the old religion abolished. The clergy were permitted to marry. Yet in this change the government of Edward had regard to the fact that the majority of the people were still Catholic. For this reason it adopted a moderate policy, intending to introduce more complete changes as the temper of the people would receive them.

Puritans.

Many of the Protestants were dissatisfied with this course, and demanded the removal of all traces of the Catholic worship. These people, who wanted the old ceremonies abolished, were called by their enemies Puritans. The refusal of Hooper to be consecrated as bishop in the robes usually worn on such occasions may be considered the beginning of Puritan history (1550).

Changes under Mary.

Edward died before the reform was completed, and Mary came to the throne (1553). She was a Catholic, and immediately filled all the church offices with men of that faith, removed from their places the clergy who had married, and fully re-established the old forms. The Protestant clergy suffered much from the zeal of the queen, and large numbers fled to the continent. Here they became still more strongly impressed in favor of a simple worship.

Policy of Elizabeth.

On the death of Mary (1558), these exiles returned to England, hoping that Elizabeth would carry on the change begun by Edward; but she found herself in a peculiar and embarrassing position. She was considered the head and exponent of Protestantism; and as such the Catholic powers of Europe were leagued against her. Many of her own subjects were ready to listen to foreign conspirators, and rise in rebellion. For this reason, though she restored the Protestants to place, she did not push the new religion beyond its position at the death of Edward.

Two laws of a preceding reign were re-enacted, and became under her administration instruments of the severest oppression. One, called the Act of Supremacy, required all ecclesiastical officers, and all officers of the government, to take an oath to support the queen as the supreme head of the Church. This, good Catholics could not do; and they lost all controlling influence from that date. Besides this, at different times, other laws were passed under which the Catholics suffered much persecution.

Act of Supremacy.

The second statute, called the Act of Uniformity, forbade worship to be conducted in any place, public or private, in any way but that prescribed by law, and required all persons to attend public service at the stated times. Under the direction of some of the bishops, this law was brought to bear upon the Puritans, who had quietly been worshipping in their own way. Hundreds of the parish clergy were expelled from their livings. From all over England complaints came to the queen, that the churches were closed, and the people deprived of the customary religious observances. The petitions were not heeded, and the persecution went on.

Act of Uniformity.

About this time, in consequence of persecution in different parts of the country, a new idea about religion was gaining favor. Some people had come to believe that the government should have no control over the religious opinions and practices of its subjects. They held that any body of

Rise of the Separatists.

Christians might organize themselves into a church, choose their own officers, and be independent of all external authority. Thus, breaking away entirely from the Established Church, they began to organize themselves by the choice of pastors, teachers, and other officers, and to worship in secret. These radical reformers were called in derision, Brownists, from an early advocate of the doctrine, who afterward went back to the state church. Afterward they were called Separatists and Independents. They were as obnoxious to the Puritans as to the government, and were punished by fines, imprisonment, torture, mutilation, and death; but they steadily increased in numbers.

Parties in Religion.

During the latter part of the reign of Elizabeth, there came to be five religious classes: the Church party, holding extreme views of the authority of the government, and sustaining all its harsh procedure; the conforming Puritans, who desired reform, yet from motives of policy or fear, or from associations, still adhered to the prescribed modes of worship; the non-conforming Puritans, who believed in the authority of the civil magistrate in matters of religion, but could not conscientiously adopt the ritual established for them, and were hoping for a change in the policy of the state; the Separatists, who had renounced the state religion, and were worshipping in little companies, in houses and barns, and wherever they could be concealed from the officers of law; and, lastly, the Catholics. An understanding of New England history requires that this distinction between the Separatists and Non-conforming Puritans be carefully noticed. The latter believed that the form of religious service should be prescribed by law, and that the civil magistrates might and should punish persons for heretical belief and practices: the other believed in the entire separation of church and state.

The Stuarts and the Popular Party.

On the accession of James (1603), the first of the Stuarts on the throne of England, the Puritans hoped for favor; but they were disappointed. Seeing nothing to hope for at home, they began that emigration by which the Puritan colonies in New England were peopled. There began now a struggle between the king, determined to exercise arbitrary power, and the Commons, who had been growing stronger, and among whom Puritans were numerous. The Commons claimed, and, after a time, succeeded in securing, the right to judge of the elections of their own members. They contended for free speech in Parliament, for the right to discuss all matters pertaining to the general interest of the kingdom, for exemption from arbitrary imprisonment, and that there should be no taxation without their assent. All these claims were resisted by James, and after him by Charles. They summoned parliaments to grant them money for carrying on the government; the Commons demanded redress of grievances as a condition of voting the supplies. This, in general, was the attitude of the two contending parties.

Petition of Right.

Early in the reign of Charles (1628), the Commons framed an instrument called the Petition of Right, to which the king unwillingly assented. In this the Commons complained of illegal and unjust procedure, and claimed four rights: first, that no person should be compelled to pay any tax levied without consent of Parliament; second, that no freeman should be imprisoned except by regular legal process; third, that soldiers should not be quartered upon the people; fourth, that the people should not be subjected to martial law. These were not new claims. The second and fourth were as old as Magna Charta; the first was older still. But *the people* now were enlightened enough and strong enough to insist upon them.

The Long Parliament. At one time, Charles governed for eleven years without a parliament, raising money by the most illegal and oppressive methods. When, in 1640, he summoned another, a majority were Puritans. They had always been foremost in opposing the absolute policy of the kings, and many of them now had come to be Independents. This Long Parliament, as it is called, because existing twelve years, carried at the outset two measures of the utmost importance in restraining the arbitrary rule of the king. One law ordained that Parliament should not be dissolved without its own consent; the other abolished the Court of Star Chamber, a body of judges wholly under the king's control, by which all the constitutional modes of administering justice had been set aside, and which had been the instrument of all the kings in disposing of obnoxious personal enemies.

The Civil War. Charles was compelled to assent to these measures; but when the parliament demanded the control of the army he resisted, and both parties took up arms (1642). The king was supported by most of the nobility, by the Catholics, and by the Church party. The parliamentary side was taken by the Puritans and by the middle and lower classes of the people. During the war the Episcopal Church was overthrown, and a Presbyterian form of worship and church government prevailed. The king finally fell into the hands of the parliament, by whom he was tried and executed for treason (1649).

The Commons then abolished the House of Lords, and vested the supreme executive power in a council of state of forty members. In 1653 Cromwell dissolved the parliament by force. Another parliament gave to him the supreme power with the title Lord Protector. He summoned and dissolved one parliament after another, ruling quite absolutely until his death in 1658. The triumph of the Commons, instead of establishing the government on a firm basis, and securing that civil and political liberty for which they had been struggling so long, only introduced a period of greater contention, of which the people became thoroughly tired.

The Commonwealth.

Cromwell was succeeded by his son Richard, who could not exercise his father's sway, and resigned his place. The control of affairs fell into the hands of a few military leaders; and in 1660 the people gladly received as king Charles II., who had been in exile during the existence of the Commonwealth. This event is known in English history as the Restoration. The government was re-established on its old basis, the episcopal system again set up, and for a time the parliament was submissive to the king; but his favor to the Catholics, and other measures, alienated the people from him. His brother James, who succeeded him (1685), attempted to re-establish the absolutism that had characterized the Tudors. He claimed the power to set aside acts of Parliament; he purposed to repeal the Habeas Corpus act, passed in the preceding reign; he wished to

The Restoration.

Arbitrary Rule of James.

establish Catholicism as the state religion; he interfered in the election of members of Parliament; and he assumed the control of ecclesiastical affairs.

The Revolution.

These arbitrary measures alarmed and exasperated the people, and after reigning four years James was compelled to fly from the country. The crown was then offered to William of Orange and his wife Mary, the daughter of James. This event is known as the Revolution (1689). Its consequences were most important.

Bill of Rights.

On the accession of William and Mary, a parliament was summoned which passed the famous Bill of Rights, which has been called the third bulwark of English liberty. The other two are Magna Charta and the Petition of Right. This bill declared it illegal for the sovereign to suspend the laws, or dispense with their execution, or to levy money without grant of Parliament, or to keep a standing army without the consent of Parliament. The bill declared the right of the subjects to petition the king, to bear arms in their own defence, to be exempt from excessive bail and fines, and from cruel and unusual punishments. It also declared that parliaments should be held frequently, that the election of members should be free, and that the members should have freedom of speech in their debates.

During this reign, considerable progress was made toward securing religious toleration and freedom of the press; and a limited term was fixed for the duration of Parliament. The mutual relations of king and Parliament became definitely settled, and the constitution has undergone but slight changes since.

SUMMARY.

1. Under the Saxon kings, the government was limited in two directions: first, by the county courts, in which the freemen administered their own local affairs; and, second, by the great council, whose consent was necessary for taxation.

2. Under the Normans, the feudal system gave more power to the crown. The arbitrary exercise of this power was the origin of the first formal declaration of civil liberty in Magna Charta.

3. The House of Commons originated in a desire of the crown to make itself independent of the nobility by creating a new party in its own interests.

4. This body acquired the right to frame statutes, to originate money bills, to examine into the public expenditure, to hold the king's ministers responsible.

5. The separation of the Church of England from Rome was effected by Henry VIII.

6. The change from the Catholic to the Protestant faith was effected during the reign of Edward VI.

7. The Puritans were Protestants who were dissatisfied with the moderate policy of reform adopted by Edward and afterward by Elizabeth, and urged the entire abolition of Catholic forms.

8. Some of the Puritans were driven by persecution to adopt new principles of ecclesiastical polity, and advocated the right of Christians to organize their own churches and choose their own officers, without dictation or control by any external authority. These people were called Separatists.

9. Most of the Puritans believed in a union of church and state.

10. The Puritans became the chief opponents of the arbitrary political measures of the Stuarts.

11. During the reign of James I and Charles I., there was a continual struggle between the Commons and the king, about taxation, and freedom of speech in Parliament. Charles assented to the Petition of Right. The quarrel ended in the civil war, in which the king was defeated, and in consequence of which he lost his life.

12. For a few years the monarchy was abolished, and the Commons ruled under the guidance of Cromwell. This was the period of the Commonwealth.

13. A reaction followed in favor of royalty: the restoration of the Stuarts took place, and liberty was again restricted.

14. Arbitrary rule again excited discontent, and brought about the Revolution, in which James II. was compelled to leave the throne, and the crown was given to William and Mary.

15. A bill of rights was passed, which became one of the chief safeguards of English liberty.

IMPORTANT DATES.

1066. Norman Conquest.
1215. Magna Charta.
1517. Lutheran Reformation.
1649. Execution of Charles I.
1660. The Restoration.
1689. The Revolution.

SOVEREIGNS OF ENGLAND.

Normans.

William I.	1066–1087.
William II.	1087–1100.
Henry I.	1100–1135.
Stephen,	1135–1154.

House of Plantagenet.

Henry II.	1154–1189.
Richard I.	1189–1199.
John,	1199–1216.
Henry III.	1216–1272.

Edward I.	1272–1307.
Edward II.	1307–1327.
Edward III.	1327–1377.
Richard II.	1377–1399.

Houses of Lancaster and York.

Henry IV.	1399–1413.
Henry V.	1413–1422.
Henry VI.	1422–1461.
Edward IV.	1461–1483.
Edward V.	1483–1483.
Richard III.	1483–1485.

House of Tudor.

Henry VII.	1485–1509.
Henry VIII.	1509–1547.
Edward VI.	1547–1553.
Mary,	1553–1558.
Elizabeth,	1558–1603.

House of Stuart.

James I.	1603–1625.
Charles I.	1625–1649.
(The Commonwealth).	
Charles II.	1660–1685.
James II.	1685–1689.

Houses of Stuart and Nassau.

William III.	1689–1702.
Mary II.	1689–1694.
Anne,	1702–1714.

House of Brunswick.

George I.	1714–1727.
George II.	1727–1760.
George III.	1760–1820.
George IV.	1820–1830.
William IV.	1830–1837.
Victoria.	1837–1900.
Edward VII.	1900–

CHAPTER IX.

THE COLONY OF NEW PLYMOUTH.

Discovery by Cabot.

In 1497, one year before Columbus discovered the continent of South America, John Cabot and his son Sebastian, sailing under the English flag, discovered the mainland of North America at Labrador, and took possession of it in the name of Henry VII. In accordance with feudal principles, the territory thus acquired became subject not to England, but to the king, who in future grants styled himself the sovereign lord thereof.

Grants by James I.

In 1606, James I. issued a patent, as it was called, granting to certain men the territory in North America between the thirty-fourth and forty-fifth degrees of latitude, extending inland fifty miles. These men were to form two companies: the London Company might occupy between the thirty-fourth and forty-first degrees; the Plymouth Company might occupy between the thirty-eighth and forty-fifth degrees; but neither could settle within a hundred miles of the other. These companies were formed for the purpose of trade and settlement. They could send out colonies, and grant land to them, could defend them against all aggressors, and had the absolute monopoly of all trade and commerce that grew out of their enterprise. The London Company planted Virginia: the other body made only unsuccessful attempts within the limits assigned them.

The Council for New England.

In 1620 the king incorporated the members of the Plymouth division of the old company into a new and distinct body called usually "The Council for New England." To this corporation was given in absolute title the territory between the fortieth and forty-eighth degrees of latitude, extending across the continent from sea to sea. The council received not only the same powers that the old company had, but the right to make all provision for governing the colonists whom they might send out. From this council were received all the titles to lands in Massachusetts, Maine, and New Hampshire.

The Pilgrim Church.

In 1608 a company of Separatists who had been worshipping according to their ideas in the village of Scrooby, in Nottinghamshire, England, were driven by persecution to fly to Holland, where religious toleration existed. They went to Amsterdam, and thence to Leyden, where they remained until 1620. Not satisfied with their condition here, they decided to emigrate to America.

Means for Emigration.

Two things were necessary: to secure a title to land, and to raise money for the expenses of the outfit. The first they obtained from the London Company, intending to settle within its grant. The king, in general terms, promised that they should be unmolested by him. They obtained funds by a partnership with some London merchants, but on terms which hindered the prosperity of the colony. Ten pounds was the price of a share in the common stock. Each settler's labor was valued at one share. If he put in ten pounds in money besides, he was entitled to two shares. The settlers and their families were to live out of the common stock for seven years; at the end of which time all lands, buildings, &c., were to be divided among the shareholders. The community of property and labor was injurious to the best interests of the settlers.

Land Grant. Instead of settling within the territory of the London Company, they found themselves at Cape Cod, and on the 21st of December, 1620, began the settlement of New Plymouth. Eight years after, they obtained from the Council for New England a grant of land with obscurely defined limits, and power to exercise such civil authority as they might find necessary.

The story of their voyage, and the hardships of their first winter, are matters of general history. The object of this chapter is to exhibit the character of their civil government.

Character of the Colony. They had existed in England and Holland as a church, and, until they reached the New World, had been nothing more than a voluntary association, organized first for religious purposes, and then for emigration. Now they were about to become a civil society, and knew that government would be necessary. They were still Englishmen, subjects of King James, and inhabitants of English soil. They were therefore amenable to the laws of England. But there existed no provision for administering those laws. They were left wholly to themselves.

They met this emergency in the spirit of their religious faith; and, by a compact adopted before their landing, forty-one of the members of the company formed themselves into a civil body politic, and agreed to choose such officers, and make such laws, as their circumstances might make necessary; and they promised submission and obedience to this rule of the whole.[1] Here was the founding of a state; not a sovereign state, because it recognized the authority of King James, but a dependent state for local government.

The Compact.

The original signers of the compact were styled freemen of the colony; and they constituted the voting population, with such persons as they by vote of the majority admitted from time to time. For many years no qualifications were specified as necessary in order to become a freeman. In 1658 it was enacted that no Quaker should become a member of their association; and in 1671 freemen were required to be twenty-one years of age, of sober and peaceable conversation, orthodox in the fundamentals of religion,

Freemen.

[1] The compact was as follows: "In the name of God, amen. We, whose names are underwritten, the loyal subjects of our dread sovereign lord, King James, by the grace of God, of Great Britain, France, and Ireland, King, Defender of the Faith, &c., having undertaken, for the glory of God, and advancement of the Christian faith, and honor of our king and country, a voyage to plant the first colony in the northern parts of Virginia, do by these presents, solemnly and mutually, in the presence of God and of one another, covenant and combine ourselves together into a civil body politic, for our better ordering and preservation, and furtherance of the ends aforesaid; and by virtue hereof to enact, constitute, and frame such just and equal laws, ordinances, acts, constitutions, and offices, from time to time, as shall be thought most meet and convenient for the general good of the colony; unto which we promise all due submission and obedience. In witness whereof we have hereunder subscribed our names, at Cape Cod, the 11th of November, in the year of the reign of our sovereign lord, King James of England, France, and Ireland, the eighteenth, and of Scotland the fifty-fourth, Anno Domini 1620."

and possessing at least twenty pounds ratable estate within the colony. These restrictions were not adopted until the generation of original settlers had passed away: *they* were always true to their Separatist ideas of religious freedom.

Form of Government. The freemen annually elected a governor, and five (afterward seven) assistants. This was the executive department. A meeting of the governor and assistants was called a Court of Assistants. A meeting of all the freemen was called a General Court. Laws were made by the general courts; and both bodies exercised judicial functions as circumstances made necessary. The first legislative act on record is the establishment of trial by jury.

Early Legislation. The early legislation was simple, and but little of it recorded. It furnishes an admirable illustration of the gradual process by which the statute law of a state is developed under the pressure of circumstances. The infant colony had suffered from scarcity of food; and a law was made prohibiting the exportation of corn, pease, and beans. The thatched roofs had taken fire; and the people were forbidden to cover their buildings with straw. Thus, as occasion required, new statutes were made; but the principles which guided their administration were those of the English common law. In 1636 a revision of the law was made; and at this time the functions of the several officers were more clearly defined.

Towns. In this code is the first formal intimation of the separation into towns. Upon the expiration of the seven years for which the partnership was formed with the London merchants, the lands were divided among the freemen, who began to extend their settlements to a considerable distance from Plymouth. In 1636 Scituate and Duxbury seem to have acquired considerable importance, as two men from each were appointed, with four from Plymouth, to revise the laws. By a new statute of this year, the inhabitants of Plymouth were permitted to meet together to make "orders for the herding of their cattle, and such other things as shall be needful for their more neighborly living together;" and it was not long before similar privileges were granted to other communities.

Representation.

By this time it had come to be inconvenient and unsafe for the freemen to leave their homes, and go to Plymouth to attend the frequent meetings of the General Court. In 1638 the representative system was established. There had come to be eight towns; and in each the inhabitants were to choose two freemen (Plymouth four) as deputies, who should act with the governor and assistants as a legislative body. The whole body of freemen still elected the officers annually, though the voters of any town might express their choice by proxy through their deputies.

Revised Laws of 1671.

In 1671 the frame of government became still more definitely established by a revision of the laws, and the publication of them under the title, "General Laws and Liberties of New Plymouth Colony." This body of laws is prefaced by a chapter entitled "The General Fundamentals." The first sections of this are important as showing what the colonists regarded as their rights. After stating that they had come hither as "freeborn subjects of the state of England," with all the privileges of such, they ordain, "that no act, imposition, law, or ordinance be made or imposed upon us, at present or to come, but such as shall be made or imposed by consent of the body of freemen or associates, or their representatives legally assembled, which is according to the free liberties of the state of England." They further declare that no person shall be governor or assistant but such as have been freely chosen by vote of the freemen. Next they assert that grand declaration of Magna Charta, that there shall be a free, impartial, and speedy administration of justice, and that no person shall be deprived of his natural rights but by due process of law. Trial by jury is also guaranteed. The growth of the colony is nowhere more manifest than in these successive revisions of the laws. By this code, the judicial functions were withdrawn from the General Court, and vested in a court of assistants, which was to sit at Plymouth at least three times a year, and which was to decide all capital, criminal, and civil causes. Beside this supreme body, in each town a body of selectmen was to be chosen; who should have the power to try all civil causes involving debt, trespass, or damage, not exceeding forty shillings. From this local judgment there might be an appeal to the assistants' court. Thus was justice "brought home to every man's door" as the English constitution demanded.

Separate Judicial Bodies.

In 1685 three counties were formed by grouping neighboring towns. They were called Plymouth, Barnstable, and Bristol. In each county two annual courts were to be held by such of the assistants, called magistrates, as lived within their limits. Much of the business that had been transacted by the courts of assistants was now placed in the hands of the county courts. At the same time full powers were given to the selectmen to attend to the local affairs

Formation of Counties.

of the town, as care of the poor, care of highways, and preservation of the public peace. In a future chapter we shall examine the functions of counties and towns in detail. This colony remained distinct until 1692, when it was united with Massachusetts.

SUMMARY.

1. All grants of lands in North America were made by the king. The title to the territory of New Plymouth was obtained from the Council for New England.

2. The settlers were a company of Separatists, who from their many wanderings have been called Pilgrims.

3. Being a voluntary association, and without civil authority, they drew up a *compact* by which they agreed to establish a government in which the members of the association should have an equal voice.

4. Members of the association were called freemen; and they were admitted by vote of the majority, at first without specified qualifications: afterward suffrage was restricted on the basis of character, religious belief, and property.

5. At first the colonists lived together at Plymouth: afterward they formed different communities which were empowered to transact local affairs. In the management of town business, persons of good character might vote, though not freemen of the colony.

6. Executive functions were in the hands of a governor and assistants, called magistrates, chosen annually by vote of a majority of the freemen.

7. Legislative functions at first were vested in the whole body of freemen acting together as a general court. Afterward the general court consisted of the magistrates, and deputies sent by the towns to represent them.

8. Judicial functions were exercised at first both by the magistrates alone and by the general court; then by the magistrates holding courts for the whole colony, and by selectmen chosen in the towns to decide small causes; afterward by county courts and the selectmen.

9. All legislation recognized the supreme authority of the king; and justice was administered according to the common law of England.

CHAPTER X.

THE COLONY OF MASSACHUSETTS BAY.

In 1628 some persons in England obtained from the Council for New England a grant of land extending from three miles north of the River Merrimack to three miles south of the Charles, and from ocean to ocean. The next year, these persons with others, being Puritans or favorably disposed toward Puritanism, and many of them men of influence at court, received a charter from the king, incorporating them under the title, "The Governor and Company of the Massachusetts Bay in New England." Their object was to found a colony where non-conforming Puritans could live and worship unmolested.

The Incorporated Company.

The charter empowered the company to choose its own officers, to admit new members, to hold land and other property in England and America, especially the territory in New England included in the previous grant, to transport settlers, to make all rules for managing the company affairs, and to provide for governing and protecting its colonists.

Powers.

The administration of company business was to be in the hands of a governor, deputy governor, and eighteen assistants, chosen annually by the whole body of freemen or members. Four times a

Government.

year, there was to be "a great, general, and solemn assembly" of the company, called "the Great and General Court," at which new members should be admitted, laws made for the government of the company and colony, and, once a year, officers chosen.

Transfer of Charter.

The company sent out a few settlers to Salem; but while its meetings were held in England, the colonists, though members of it, had no voice in its management. Men of character and influence were unwilling thus to deprive themselves of the privilege of self-government, and would not emigrate. To remove this objection, it was soon decided to transfer the charter to New England; and a large body of settlers immediately came over, locating themselves in Boston and vicinity about 1630. The effect of the change was, to give the control of the colony to those settlers who were members of the company. The others had no more voice than before. But the company had changed to a body politic. To be a freeman of the company was to be a citizen; and thus, as new members were admitted from time to time, the colony came to be self-governing under the protection of the company charter. Very early it was enacted that no person could become a freeman unless he were a member of some church within the colony; and this provision remained in force until 1664.

Freemen.

Government.

The administration of government, both executive and judicial, was intrusted to the governor and assistants, sometimes called magistrates, who held monthly meetings called Assistants' Courts. The whole company in its general courts, held somewhat irregularly, chose officers, made laws, and attended to some judicial business. The records show that at first the functions were not very clearly defined.

In 1634 the towns sent deputies to act with the magistrates; and for ten years these two bodies, sitting together but voting separately, formed the General Court for legislative business. No law could be enacted without a majority vote of both bodies, each having what is called a "negative" upon the other. In 1644 the two bodies were separated; and thus the General Court was constituted for forty years. At first the whole people met for election: afterward they met in their towns and voted, and sent their votes by their deputies to be counted by the General Court.

Representatives.

Judicial business, as has been said, was conducted both by the Court of Assistants and by the General Court. Very early the magistrates performed the functions of justices of the peace, though without the title. Soon four quarterly courts were established at Ipswich, Salem, Cambridge, and Boston, to be held by the resident magistrates, and persons appointed by the General Court to act with them; and a quarterly court at Boston by all the magistrates. Next, in each town, a magistrate, or some person appointed for the purpose, was empowered to try cases involving less than twenty shillings. In 1643 four counties were organized for the more complete administration of justice.

Very early the people formed the habit of meeting in the towns to discuss local matters, and of choosing men to manage them; and it was not long before the General Court recognized the town as corporations, and gave them power to transact business, and to choose officers.

Towns.

Puritan Legislation.

The Puritan settlers of Massachusetts Bay, unlike the Pilgrims, believed that the civil magistrate had authority in matters pertaining to religion and the church. They had founded their state for the express purpose of maintaining what they believed to be a pure worship; and much of the legislation was directed to securing this end. This was the reason for restricting suffrage to church-members. In furtherance of the same object, they endeavored to compel attendance upon all the stated religious services, and taxed all the inhabitants to support the gospel. They passed stringent laws to prevent the promulgation of what they considered erroneous views, and punished severely any attempt to introduce a different faith from that which they had devoted themselves to establish. They endeavored to promote the public morals by legislation respecting the observance of the Sabbath; and numerous statutes were made to prevent profanity, intemperance, and impiety. Most of the other New England colonies copied these laws; and the reputation which these states have always had for morality shows how successful was this early legislation.

Demand of Charles II.

After the Restoration, Charles II., who had no love for Puritans, was disturbed by the progress of this colony, and began a series of measures to check what seemed a dangerous spirit of independence. He required the officers to take an oath of allegiance to him; that all judicial processes should be issued in his name; that the Episcopal form of worship should be tolerated; and that the rights of freemen should not be restricted to church-members. The colonists considered some of these demands to be contrary to the terms of their charter, and withheld compliance.

Next, the king sent commissioners to investigate the state of the colonies, giving them power to hear any complaints that might be made against the colonial governments, and to receive appeals from the colonial courts. They were also directed to use their influence to induce the colonies to give up their charters, and receive a royal governor. Most of the colonies received the commissioners, and treated them with consideration; but Massachusetts refused to acknowledge their authority, and would not allow any appeal to them.

Royal Commissioners.

The king continued his demands, to some of which Massachusetts yielded, imposing the oath of allegiance upon all the freemen, modifying some of the severest laws against the Quakers, and repealing the act limiting suffrage to church-members. But she required that voters who were not church-members should be orthodox in religion, not vicious in life, twenty-four years of age, householders, and paying a yearly tax upon property so great that practically the franchise was scarcely extended beyond its old limits.

Extension of Suffrage.

At length the struggle ended by a legal declaration on the part of the king's officers, that Massachusetts had forfeited her charter. This was in 1684, and measures were at once taken to send out a royal governor; but the death of the king prevented.

Loss of the Charter.

James, his successor, whose arbitrary conduct drove the people of England to revolution, was not likely to treat the New England colonies with much favor; and for a time popular government there was suspended. In 1686 the

Suspension of Popular Government.

king appointed a president, deputy president, and sixteen councillors, to have complete executive and judicial control over Massachusetts, New Hampshire, and Maine. There was no provision for an assembly. Near the close of the same year, Sir Edmund Andros arrived in Boston as governor of all New England. When the charter of Massachusetts was revoked, all powers which it conferred were withdrawn, and the colony was left wholly at the mercy of the king. Even the titles to land, based upon the charter, were void. The people were considered subjects not of England, but of the *king* of England, and therefore not entitled to the civil and political rights of Englishmen.

Government of Andros.

Andros was sent to put these principles into practice. A council appointed by the king was associated with him; and together they were empowered to make laws, which should be sent to England for the royal sanction, to levy taxes, to establish courts of justice, to regulate trade and currency, to reprieve and pardon. The servant was as tyrannical as his master. Excessive taxes were imposed; and, though the people resisted, they were compelled to pay them. Owners of land were required to pay certain sums, called quit-rents, in order to secure a new and valid title to their property. The council became a cipher in the administration, and the will of Andros became the sole law; and he and his favorites enriched themselves at the expense of the people. In the next year, his commission was extended to include New York and New Jersey; and Boston was made the capital of the whole province. Early in 1689, news arrived of the dethronement of James, and the accession of William and Mary. At once there was an uprising of the people of Boston.

Andros and his friends were seized and imprisoned, and a provincial government was established on the basis of the old charter. Similar proceedings took place in Plymouth, and in Rhode Island and Connecticut, which had never given up their charters.

Revolution of 1689.

The agents of Massachusetts tried in vain to secure a renewal of the old charter. Its provisions were too liberal to suit the king; and in 1691 a new one was made, known as the Province Charter. The terms of this were such that the people no longer had that virtual independence of the crown which they had so long enjoyed, and which their neighbors of Connecticut and Rhode Island still possessed. Massachusetts, Plymouth, Maine, and Nova Scotia were united under one government. A governor, deputy, and secretary were to be appointed by the king. A house of deputies, chosen as before by the towns, and a council of twenty-eight members, appointed at first by the king, afterward by the General Court, formed the legislature. The governor was commander of the militia, and appointed all military officers. The election of councillors was subject to his sanction. With the consent of the council he appointed all judicial officers. The General Court was to assemble on the last Wednesday in May, and the governor could convoke, adjourn, or dissolve it. This dangerous power was afterward used against the people when they were preparing for the Revolution. All acts passed by the deputies and council must receive the approval of the governor to become law, and then be sent to England for the approval of the king's ministers. They could be

The Province Charter.

Change in the Government.

annulled within three years. Much of the first legislation failed to receive the royal sanction.

The General Court established a new judiciary system, consisting of a superior court, a court of common pleas in each county, justices of the peace, and a court of sessions in each county, consisting of the justices of the peace therein, who heard appeals from the justice's courts, and had charge of some miscellaneous county business. The charter changed the basis of suffrage, making the qualifications for a freeman the possession of a freehold[1] worth two pounds sterling a year, or personal property worth forty pounds. This charter went into operation in 1692; and from that time until the Revolution, Massachusetts and Plymouth, having lost the privilege of self-government, existed as a royal province subject to such governors as the king of England chose to send.

SUMMARY.

1. The Massachusetts Bay Colony was established under a charter from Charles I., in Boston and vicinity, about 1630.

2. The control of the colony was vested in the company; but by a transfer of the charter the power came into the hands of a portion of the settlers.

3. Executive and judicial power was chiefly exercised by a governor, deputy governor, and assistants. Legislative functions were exercised by the whole body of members of the company, meeting in an assembly called the Great and General Court. At this meeting, also, officers were chosen.

[1] Freehold, — an estate held in absolute ownership, either for life or without limitation of time.

4. Different communities early assumed the powers of towns, which powers were afterward formally confirmed by the court.

5. In a few years, these towns chose deputies to act with the assistants in legislation; and the General Court came to consist of two bodies, each having a negative upon the other.

6. Judicial business was gradually withdrawn from the General Court, and intrusted to courts held in different parts of the colony by the magistrates, afterward to county courts; and persons in the towns were empowered to "end small causes."

7. Only church-members were allowed to become freemen; and thus the political power was in the hands of a small minority of the colonists. The legislation was also largely in the interests of the Puritan churches.

8. The kings were displeased with the practical independence of this colony, and tried various means to reduce it to subjection. Finally, in 1686, the charter was taken away, and with it all political privileges.

9. During several years the colony was under the control of persons sent from England. These were intrusted with extensive authority, which they abused; and the people had no means of redress.

10. The Revolution in England was followed by a similar outbreak in Massachusetts. On the accession of William and Mary, a new charter, called the Province Charter, was given to the people.

11. This gave the choice of governor to the king, of judges to the governor, of deputies to the people, and of a council to the General Court, which consisted of deputies and council. The people lost much of the

power which they enjoyed under the company charter. At this time Plymouth was united with Massachusetts.

12. New courts were established, suffrage was based upon a property qualification, and the king's assent was required to all laws.

CHAPTER XI.

THE COLONIES OF CONNECTICUT AND RHODE ISLAND.

CONNECTICUT.

Grant of Territory. As in the other colonies, the title to the territory occupied by Connecticut was based upon a grant of land from the Council for New England. This was made to its president the Earl of Warwick, who deeded it to a company of eleven persons, of whom Lord Say and Seal was the first named. The limits of the grant were, on the east, the Narragansett River; on the north, a straight line from that river westerly; on the south, the seashore for one hundred and twenty miles; on the west, the South Sea. Within these limits, a number of detached companies settled themselves, but soon became united into two colonies.

The Connecticut Colony. About 1635 settlers from the vicinity of Boston emigrated to the Connecticut River, and located themselves at Windsor, Wethersfield, and Hartford. They supposed themselves to be within the territory of Massachusetts; and the General Court granted a commission to eight of the prominent men to govern the colony for one year. These men seem to have administered all the colony affairs for about three years. Sometimes, when special business made it advisable, the towns appointed committees to act with the court.

The Constitution. In 1639 all the free planters met at Hartford, and framed and adopted a constitution, which is considered the first instrument of the kind on record. It provided for two general courts annually: one for election, where the whole body of freemen were to choose by ballot a governor and six magistrates, or assistants; the other court, for legislation, was to consist of four deputies from each of the original towns, and from new towns according to the population, with the governor and magistrates. The governor had power to convoke the assemblies; but they could only be adjourned or dissolved by vote of a majority of the members. Judicial powers were in the hands of the magistrates. In this instrument there was no recognition of any external authority whatever. The first court held after the adoption of the constitution prepared a bill of rights which in its main provision was based upon Magna Charta.

Towns. In the same year, each town was empowered to dispose of its own lands, to choose its own officers, and order its own local affairs. In each, three, five, or seven men might be chosen annually, who should have power to decide all controversies when the amount at issue did not exceed forty shillings. A town clerk was also to be chosen.

New Haven Colony. In 1638 a company of persons from England, under the lead of John Davenport and Theophilus Eaton, formed a settlement at New Haven. It was a wealthy society, and so united and well disposed that there was no civil, military, or ecclesiastical authority for the first year. Then, at a meeting of the people, it was agreed, that church-members only should be freemen, and they only should choose magistrates. They therefore proceeded to choose twelve men, who of their own number selected seven to begin the church. These seven, called pillars, formed the church out of such individuals as they saw fit. The church so formed, with such members of other churches as desired, constituted the body of freemen; and they elected a governor and four magistrates. Legislative or judicial business was transacted both by the magistrates, and by the general court of all the freemen.

Settlements were soon after made at Milford, Guilford, and Stamford; and each town governed itself after the New Haven model. In 1643 these four towns united under a form essentially the same as in the Connecticut Colony. In all, the state was ruled by the church, as in Massachusetts Bay.

The Charter Government.

The two colonies remained distinct until 1662, when a charter was obtained from the king incorporating nineteen persons of Connecticut, with such associates as they might elect, under the title, "The Governor and Company of the English Colony of Connecticut in New England in America." The territory granted them embraced that formerly given to Warwick, and included the towns of the New Haven Colony. There was to be a governor, deputy governor, and twelve assistants, and a house of deputies composed of two members from each town; all elected annually by the freemen. As in most of the other charters, there was a reservation that no laws should be made repugnant to the laws of England.

This patent was exceedingly obnoxious to the people of New Haven, who by it would lose their separate existence, and with it the fundamental principle upon which their government was based. The privilege of becoming freemen could no longer be restricted to church-members. For three years New Haven refused to accede to the demand of Connecticut, and maintained its independence; but in 1665 it was obliged to yield, and the charter government went into operation. So completely was the power in the hands of the people that even the Revolution made no change necessary, and this charter formed the only constitution of Connecticut until 1818.

Counties. For the administration of justice, courts were held in the counties by the resident assistants, from whose judgment appeals might be made to the Assistants' Court at Hartford, which also had jurisdiction in all capital cases. The pardoning power was vested in the general assembly.

Legislation. The legislation was, in the main, copied from the Massachusetts code, and was not less minute in its provisions to promote Sabbath-keeping, chastity, and temperance; but the so-called Blue Laws, with their absurd details, were the invention of a man not in sympathy with the colony, who had returned to England.

Suffrage. The right of suffrage was granted to any person twenty-one years of age, owning real estate to the amount of twenty pounds, and recommended by the selectmen of his town as of honest, civil, and peaceable conversation.

RHODE ISLAND.

Providence Plantation. As in Connecticut, so in Rhode Island, various isolated settlements were at first made, which soon found it necessary to unite for mutual protection. In 1636 Roger Williams and five others began a settlement at Providence. They were soon joined by others; and Williams, who had received a deed from Indian chiefs, divided the land equally between himself and his associates. From the incomplete records of the town, it appears that the people met monthly to determine matters of general interest, but delegated no power except to a clerk and a treasurer. There is a record of an early compact in which the signers agreed to subject themselves "only in civil things" to such orders as should be made by the majority of the masters of families inhabiting the town. This limitation of the civil authority to "civil things" is characteristic of all the legislation of this colony.

Early Government.

Within a few years (1640), it became necessary to have a more complete civil organization, and it was determined to choose five "disposers," as they were called, to attend to the general business of the town. They were to meet by themselves monthly, and quarterly were to report to the town, and give up their trust for a new election. Instead of making these selectmen judges, as was done in the other colonies, all private disputes were to be settled by arbitrators chosen by the parties to the quarrel, or, if they refused, by the "disposers." Special town meetings could be called at the request of any citizen who was dissatisfied with the action of the selectmen. This was the most completely democratic government in New England. In fact, it was too democratic to work successfully. It allowed too much liberty to individuals, and gave too little authority to the community.

Rhode Island Plantation.

In 1638 a settlement was made at Portsmouth, and in the next year one at Newport; both by people from Massachusetts who, like Williams and his friends, had left that colony to escape from the intolerance of the ruling class. In these two towns the business was transacted in general meetings. Soon a judge and elders were chosen, whose official duties corresponded with those of the selectmen in the other colonies; and provision was also made for trial by jury. Frequent meetings of the townsmen were held. In 1640 the two towns united; and a general government was established, consisting of a governor, deputy governor, and assistants, chosen annually by the freemen. Provision was made for a regular administration of justice; and the official positions, and the meetings for election and of the general court, were shared equally by the two towns.

The Charter Government.

In 1644 Williams obtained from the English Parliament a charter uniting the three towns for the purpose of government, empowering them to adopt such form, and to choose such officers and make such laws, as they saw fit. After a delay of three years, they organized a government similar to that in the other colonies, but could not agree, and soon separated. In 1663 Charles II. granted another charter more explicit in its details, but giving to the people the most perfect liberty in election of officers and in legislation, and establishing complete religious toleration. The administration was to be in the hands of a governor, deputy governor, and assistants, who were to hold courts at Providence and Newport for judicial business. The towns were to choose deputies to the general court; and these with the magistrates formed the legislature. As in Connecticut, the people were so completely independent that the revolution added nothing to their political privileges; and this charter formed the only constitution until 1842.

SUMMARY.

1. The title to the territory of Connecticut was based on a grant to the Earl of Warwick by the Council for New England; and the land was purchased from the Indians.

2. There were originally two principal colonies, each a group of towns. The Connecticut colony was founded by emigrants from near Boston; the New Haven colony, by persons from England.

3. The Connecticut colony was at first governed by a Massachusetts commission, afterward under a constitution prepared by itself, which organized a representative government after the Massachusetts model, but did not make church-membership necessary to suffrage.

4. The New Haven colony started with the idea that the church should control the state, and therefore gave the suffrage only to church-members. Its form of government was essentially the same as in the other colonies.

5. The two colonies were united by a royal charter, which placed all political power in the hands of the people. The organization was the same as had previously existed in the Connecticut colony; and the conditions of suffrage were the same.

6. Towns existed from the beginning with powers of local administration.

7. Rhode Island at first existed as two colonies known as the Rhode Island and Providence Plantations.

8. Providence was founded by Roger Williams, who had been sent away from Massachusetts Bay; and Newport and Portsmouth by Coddington and others, who were also exiles.

9. The founders established the most perfect equality, vesting but little authority in any officers. It was a fundamental article in all their compacts and laws, that the government should control the people "only in civil things."

10. The different towns at first governed themselves, but were afterwards united, first by a parliamentary charter, and afterwards by one from the king.

11. Under the last charter, absolute religious freedom was secured, and a representative government wholly in the hands of the people was organized.

12. In the charters of Rhode Island and Connecticut, no authority was reserved by the king; and they therefore formed the constitution of the States until some time after the Revolution.

CHAPTER XII.

THE COLONIES OF NEW HAMPSHIRE AND MAINE.

NEW HAMPSHIRE.

Settlements.

IN 1622 the Council for New England made a grant of land between the Merrimack, the Kennebec, the ocean, and the River of Canada, to two men, Gorges and Mason; who called their territory Laconia. Under their direction, the next year, a few persons settled on the Piscataqua at Portsmouth and at Dover; but it was several years before either colony acquired much importance. In 1633 a small company of people from England settled at Dover; and, a few years after, some disaffected people from Massachusetts joined them. There was great diversity of religious opinion, and much contention. New proprietors claimed the territory, and employed agents to govern the people; but in 1640 the settlers formed a combination for self-government. A short time before this, Exeter had been founded by people from Massachusetts, — a part of the same class that settled the Rhode Island Plantation. Here a church was founded, and a form of government set up; a governor being chosen, and the whole body making laws. In 1638 Hampton was settled under the authority of the Massachusetts Court; and the next year it was empowered to act as a town, and to send a deputy to the legislature.

Massachusetts, under her charter, claimed the territory occupied by these four towns. To be free from domestic disturbance and contested claims, in 1641 a portion of the patentees of Dover and Portsmouth ceded to Massachusetts the jurisdiction over their territory. She accepted the grant, and took measures for administering the government. Persons who were freemen before the union were allowed to vote, and hold office, though not church-members; and two deputies were sent to the General Court. In 1643, on petition of the inhabitants, Exeter was received under the Massachusetts government; and in the same year all the towns north of the Merrimack were formed into a county called Norfolk. Local justice was administered as in the other parts of Massachusetts.

Cession to Massachusetts.

New Hampshire remained thus a part of Massachusetts until 1679; when it was declared by the English government a royal province, and a president and council were appointed by the king. These persons were to have judicial functions, subject to an appeal to the king; and, with an assembly of deputies from the towns, might make laws, also subject to the approval of the king. At the first meeting after the organization of the government, a code of laws was framed; in which it was declared that "no act, imposition, law, or ordinance should be made, or imposed upon them, but such as should be made by the assembly, and approved by the president and council."

Made a Royal Province.

This government, so favorable to the people, was soon superseded by one which was oppressive in the extreme. A new governor was appointed, with increased power. He might adjourn or

Oppressive Administration.

dissolve the assembly at his pleasure, might appoint all military and judicial officers, constitute judicial courts, and remove members of the council.

The people were perpetually harassed by the claims of Mason and his heirs, who demanded the payment of quit-rents, and in whose interests the governors were appointed, — men whose only object was to enrich themselves at the expense of the colony. There was much trouble between the people and their officers until the establishment of the royal government over Massachusetts, when New Hampshire was included under the administration of Dudley and afterward of Andros. All the colonies suffered alike from the tyranny of this man.

Re-Union to Massachusetts.

After the revolution, which left New England without government, the four towns which still constituted New Hampshire were at their request again united to Massachusetts (1690), and represented in its General Court. They would have chosen to remain in this condition; but the English government, always willing to curtail the power of Massachusetts, declined to sanction the union; and, when the Province charter was given (1691), New Hampshire was not included. She was again placed under a governor and council appointed by the crown, with whom were associated the usual assembly of deputies. During most of the time until the Revolution, New Hampshire and Massachusetts had the same royal governors. These usually resided in Boston, leaving the administration of affairs in the smaller province to their lieutenants.

Again Separated.

In the early part of the eighteenth century, the settlements were extended towards the west, and north as far as Concord, numbers of people from the north of Ireland settling Londonderry and the adjacent towns.

MAINE.

Kennebec Settlement. In 1628 the Council for New England gave to the colony of New Plymouth a grant of land on the Kennebec; and they proceeded to erect a trading-house. In 1652 Parliament confirmed and extended the grant. In 1654 the government of Plymouth sent a commissioner thither to organize a local government. About twenty persons took an oath of fidelity to the government of Plymouth, and chose an assistant to act with the commissioner in judicial matters. A brief code of laws was promulgated, which, among other things, provided for trial by jury, and also that capital crimes should be tried at Plymouth. It was not long before the territory was sold.

Gorges' Province. Under the early patents granted to Mason and Gorges, small settlements had been made at Saco and York; but it was not until 1639 that any thing worthy the name of government existed. In that year Gorges received a new charter as Lord Proprietary of the Province of Maine. The territory was to extend from the Piscataqua to the Kennebec, and from the ocean to a line drawn between the two rivers at a distance of one hundred and twenty miles from their mouths.

Proprietary Government. The form of government which the charter proposed was quite monarchical. Power was given to the proprietor to establish churches, organize courts, appoint all kinds of officers, make war, regulate trade, and, with representatives of the people, make laws. He might also grant lands subject to such conditions as he chose. He proceeded to organize his government by appointing a deputy governor and a council. He divided his territory into two counties, in each of which was a court, and from which deputies were chosen to the legislature. To York was given a city charter which authorized the citizens to choose a mayor, aldermen, and council, and the usual subordinate officers. Palfrey says, "Probably as many as two-thirds of the adult males were in places of authority;" and he describes the whole as "grave foolery." In a few years Saco was separated from the Province, and settlements were made at Wells and Kittery. In 1649 the inhabitants of those towns, finding themselves with a pompous form of government but no substance, met at York, and formed a body politic, choosing officers to govern them.

Acquisition of Territory by Massachusetts.

About this time Massachusetts had learned that all this territory came within the limits of her patent, and set about acquiring jurisdiction. The General Court sent three commissioners to Kittery; which after some hesitation, in 1652, submitted, and was constituted a town of Massachusetts. Its inhabitants were allowed to become freemen, without the religious qualifications; and they sent two deputies to the General Court. York followed the example of Kittery, and received the same privilege. The other three towns soon gave up their claims to independence; and all were united into a county called York. In a few years Massachusetts extended her jurisdiction to Casco Bay.

Things remained in this condition for about twenty years; when Massachusetts, finding that the English government did not recognize the validity of her title, bought the province, and thus assumed a new relation.

Massachusetts becomes Proprietor.

Gorges transferred to Massachusetts the extensive powers conferred by his charter; and Maine, instead of being a part, became only a dependency of her sister State. In 1680 Massachusetts established a provincial government. It was to consist of a president appointed annually by the governor and assistants of Massachusetts, and a legislature. This was to consist of a standing council appointed by Massachusetts, and an assembly of deputies from the towns.

Union with Massachusetts.

This arrangement was of short duration. Massachusetts soon lost her own independence, and with it all power as Lord Proprietary. Under the administration of Dudley and Andros, Maine experienced the same hardships as the other New England colonies. The Province charter of 1691 again united the two colonies; and from that time until 1820 the history of Maine is merged in that of Massachusetts.

SUMMARY.

1. The territory between the Merrimack and Kennebec was granted to Gorges and Mason in 1622. The first settlements were at Portsmouth and Dover. They were small, and had little government.

2. Exeter was settled by Massachusetts dissenters, and was self-governing. Hampton was settled under the authority of Massachusetts, and governed like the other Massachusetts towns.

3. Massachusetts acquired jurisdiction over all these places. They were formed into a county, and sent deputies to the General Court.

4. In 1679 New Hampshire was made a royal prov-

ince, with a president and council appointed by the king. An assembly of deputies was to represent the people. This government became burdensome and obnoxious; and the rule of Andros was not less so.

5. After the revolution of 1689, New Hampshire united itself again to Massachusetts, but by the provincial charter of 1691 was separated, having the same governor, but a distinct assembly.

6. New Plymouth owned a tract of land on the Kennebec, which she governed by commissioners. It was soon sold.

7. A portion of territory between the Piscataqua and Kennebec, and extending inland one hundred and twenty miles, was granted to Gorges, and called the Province of Maine. He set up a government, appointing a governor and council, and forming two counties from which deputies were sent to a legislature. York and Saco were the principal towns.

8. The towns were soon left to govern themselves; and Massachusetts claimed and acquired the jurisdiction over them, governing them like her own towns.

9. Massachusetts bought the Province from Gorges, and thus became Proprietor. She established a provincial government, which existed until Massachusetts lost her own independence; when the two were united, and remained one until 1820.

CHAPTER XIII.

THE NEW-ENGLAND CONFEDERACY.

Its Foundation.

NOT only did the New-England colonies lay broad and strong the foundations of local and individual governments, but they also inaugurated the policy of union. In 1643 articles of confederation were drawn up and adopted by the four colonies of Massachusetts, Plymouth, Connecticut, and New Haven. They gave as reasons for the act, the disturbed condition of affairs in the mother country, and the troublesome character of their neighbors. There was evidently the purpose to prepare for the worst in case the opening conflict between their enemy the king, and their friends the Parliament, should result unfavorably to the Puritan cause. The measure was certainly an assumption of a degree of sovereignty to which, as subjects of England, they had no claim. When, after the Restoration, their enemies endeavored to prejudice the king against them, they pointed to this league as conclusive evidence that the colonies meditated independence.

Nature of the Union.

The four colonies were bound together in a league of friendship for offence and defence, for mutual advice and succor in preserving and propagating their religious faith, and for their mutual safety and welfare. The name of the confederacy was The United Colonies of New England. No new member could be admitted to the union, nor could two of the colonies be united, without the consent of the rest; and each colony was to be independent within its own limits.

Commissioners.

The business of the confederacy was intrusted to commissioners, — two from each colony. No action could be taken without the concurrence of six members of the board. If so many could not agree, the business was referred to the general courts of the colonies for decision. This board chose its own president, who had no powers beyond those of any presiding officer. The meetings were held annually, or oftener, in the principal towns in the colonies.

War Quotas.

For carrying on war, supplies of men and means were furnished in proportion to the number of male inhabitants between the ages of sixteen and sixty in the respective colonies. The spoils taken in war were distributed in the same proportion. In case of the invasion of any one of the colonies, the others sent aid on request of the local magistrates. If but little aid was needed, only the nearest confederate was called upon; but Massachusetts might be required to send at once one hundred armed men with provision, and each of the others forty-five men. No larger draft could be made until a meeting of the commissioners had been held, when they might call for such troops as they deemed necessary.

General Powers.

The articles authorized the commissioners to frame such agreements and orders as should promote peace between the colonies by securing justice to the citizens of the different jurisdictions, by adopting a uniform policy towards the Indians, and by restoring runaway servants and fugitives from justice. No colony might engage in war, and thus endanger its associates, without the consent of six commissioners. A breach of the articles of confederation by any member of the league was to be considered by the commissioners of the others, who should determine the course to be pursued.

Adoption of the Articles.

These articles were adopted by the General Court of Massachusetts, and by the commissioners from New Haven and Connecticut, and were submitted by the General Court of Plymouth to the townships of the colony; by each of which they were ratified. Rhode Island was denied admittance to the union, on the ground that its territory belonged to Plymouth. It is estimated that the population of the four colonies at this time was almost twenty-four thousand; of which Massachusetts had fifteen thousand, Connecticut and Plymouth each three thousand, and New Haven twenty-five hundred.

Dissensions in the Confederacy.

While the commissioners met frequently, and made suggestions respecting such matters as have been mentioned, the inherent weakness of the confederacy was shown in the controversy with Massachusetts about a war with the Dutch. New Haven was troubled by the demands of her neighbors of New Netherlands, and suspected that the Dutch governor was inciting the Indian tribes to a general war upon the English colonies. On the strength of this suspicion, she appealed to the commissioners, who proposed to declare war. The General Court of Massachusetts, knowing that that colony would be obliged to bear the largest part of the expense, refused to be governed by the action of the commissioners, declaring that the articles of confederation gave them power only in defensive warfare, and that no agreement could bind a colony to perform an act which her conscience told her was wrong. The other colonies protested against the action of Massachusetts, accusing her of violating her faith; but she was firm in her refusal to be forced into what she thought a causeless war. After several months spent in angry discussion, the matter was settled by partial concession on both sides. But things had taken a more peaceable turn: there was now no occasion for war, and Massachusetts gained her point. The whole affair showed that any of the colonies might at pleasure disregard the voice of the commissioners, and that they could do no more than recommend and advise.

Cause of Dissolution.

The same weakness appeared when Connecticut obtained her charter, which gave her jurisdiction over New Haven. The articles of confederation stipulated that no two members should be united without the consent of all. New Haven protested against the demand of Connecticut, that she should surrender her independence; and she was sustained by Massachusetts and Plymouth. But Connecticut insisted, and finally carried her point, thus virtually dissolving the confederacy (1665).

A Second Union.

After several years, a new and similar league was formed between Massachusetts, Plymouth, and Connecticut. The only business of importance transacted by this second confederacy was the management of King Philip's war. When James II. overthrew the popular governments in New England, this colonial union perished; to be succeeded by a more enduring one when the general safety was endangered, not by neighboring savages, but by England itself.

SUMMARY.

1. In 1643 the colonies of Massachusetts, Plymouth, Connecticut, and New Haven formed a league for mutual counsel and aid.

2. The business of the union was intrusted to two commissioners from each colony.

3. In case of invasion of any colony, the others were to assist with men and means. The colonies were to furnish supplies in proportion to their fighting population.

4. There was no power in the confederacy to compel obedience to the decisions of the commissioners.

5. The league came to an end in 1665, by the union of New Haven with Connecticut.

6. A second league was formed by the three colonies, and by it King Philip's war was carried on.

CHAPTER XIV.

THE COLONIES OF NEW YORK AND NEW JERSEY.

NEW YORK.

Settlements.

AFTER Henry Hudson had explored the river which bears his name, in 1609, Dutch merchants sent vessels to trade with the Indians, and established an agency for the purpose on Manhattan Island. In 1615 they formed a company, and received from the government of Holland the monopoly of the trade for four years. They established another trading-post near the present site of Albany, and erected rude forts at both places; but the settlers were few. In 1621 the West India Company was formed, with more extensive powers both for trade and colonization. They sent a considerable body of people to Albany, and, soon after, still more to the settlement on Manhattan, which they called New Amsterdam. The whole territory between the Connecticut and the Delaware they called New Netherlands.

Government by the Dutch.

The administration of affairs was intrusted to an officer styled director-general, appointed by the home government, and a council appointed in the same way. This body acted both as an executive council and as a judicial court. In 1629 special inducements were offered for the purpose of promoting settlements. Any person who, within four years, would bring into the colony fifty persons over fifteen years of age, was promised the title "patroon," a large grant of land, and extensive commercial privileges, with complete civil and criminal jurisdiction throughout his domain. At the same time, actual settlers, emigrating at their own expense, were promised as much land as they could cultivate. Under this provision two classes of settlements arose. Large tracts of land were taken up by the patroons, and communities established under their control. They appointed local officers for administrative and judicial business. From their decision appeals might be made to the governor and council. The settlers had no political and few civil rights.

Patroons.

Numerous bodies of free settlers formed communities along the Hudson in New Jersey, and on Long Island. Such local officers as sheriffs, clerks, and magistrates, were appointed for these by the director and council, to whom appeals could be made from the local courts. For the first thirty years, the people seem to have had no voice either in the local or general government; and they frequently quarrelled with the governors about questions of authority. Sometimes the right of appeal from the director to Holland was denied; and the exercise of authority was always arbitrary and often oppressive. Justice was administered according to the common law of Holland and the enactments of the West India Company and the director-general. At different times, the governor summoned a few men from some of the larger communities to consult with the council about Indian affairs. In 1653 New Amsterdam was

Local Administration.

incorporated after the manner of Dutch towns, and a board of aldermen and magistrates were appointed by the governor. During the next ten years, the communities acquired some new powers by being allowed to choose double the number of persons required for the local officers; from whom the governor selected those who should serve as magistrates. Many English towns on Long Island had organized themselves after the New England model.

Popular Dissatisfaction.

The people came to be dissatisfied with the small share which they had in the administration, but could get no satisfaction from the governors or from the company. At one time they sent a remonstrance to the government of Holland, setting forth the grievances of the province, and citing the example of New England, "where neither patroons, nor lords, nor princes are known; but only the people." Thus it appears that the independent spirit of New England was contagious; and, throughout the colonial period, whenever any people wished for more extended liberties, they cited the prosperity of New England as an argument in favor of local self-government. Any remonstrance to the company was answered by an order to the governor to suppress sedition, and to punish the complainants in an exemplary manner.

Conquest by the English.

The English government never recognized the claim of the Dutch to land in North America; and in 1664 King Charles gave to his brother, the Duke of York, all the territory of New Netherlands, including Long Island, Martha's Vineyard, Nantucket, the Hudson River, and the land from the west side of the Connecticut River to the east side of Delaware Bay. The same royal commissioners who came to examine the charter governments of New England, and who were treated so unceremoniously in Massachusetts, were empowered to demand the surrender of the Dutch territory. The people made no resistance, and the Duke of York became proprietor of New Netherlands. This relation gave to him the exclusive right to the soil, to the revenues, and to the control of the civil administration.

Proprietary Government.

The people expected an improvement in their political condition; but it was nearly twenty years before their share in the provincial government was extended. The proprietor appointed a governor and council; and in their hands were the executive, legislative, and supreme judicial functions. The towns were authorized to choose a constable and a board of overseers, who managed the local affairs; and there was a justice of the peace appointed by the governor, who presided at the town courts. There was a county court which held jury trials, and from which in important cases appeals might be made to a supreme court called the "court of assize," held once a year, and composed of the governor, council, and town magistrates. All men who took the oath of allegiance to the proprietor, and were not servants or laborers, and owned a town lot, were freemen.

Representative Assembly.

For nearly twenty years, the proprietor refused all requests to call an assembly of the people, and continued to burden them with taxes which they had no voice in levying. At length, in 1683, he yielded to their entreaties and to the advice of friends, and instructed his governor to call an assembly. This body consisted of the governor and council, and seventeen deputies elected by the freeholders.

A charter of liberties was prepared, which at length brought the colony into line with those about it. It declared that supreme legislative power should forever remain vested in the governor, council, and people, met in general assembly. Every freeholder and freeman might vote without restraint for representatives. No tax should be assessed without the consent of the assembly. Trial by jury was established, and religious toleration declared. The governor had a veto on all acts of the assembly; and the duke might reject any law. On the accession of the proprietor to the throne of England as James II., these privileges were revoked; and New York was governed like the New England colonies, without an assembly.

Charter of Liberties.

On the accession of William and Mary, the people elected deputies from the counties, who met in assembly with the new governor, and re-organized the government. They established a revenue, organized a judiciary, and declared the right of the people to a voice in the administration. The latter provision was repealed by the king; but practically, from this time, the legislative department was constituted as in the other provinces. As in New England, from this time to the declaration of independence there was a continual struggle between the assembly and the royal governor concerning their respective powers. The question of salaries was especially vexing. After a time the assembly established the practice of making special appropriations for each purpose of government, and making these only for a year at a time. The government retained its form until the Revolution, the people exhibiting the same spirit in resisting British encroachments that marked the other colonies.

Permanent Government.

NEW JERSEY.

First Proprietor. The territory now occupied by New Jersey had been a part of the province of New Netherlands, and in its northern parts was occupied by a few scattering Dutch families. It was included in the grant made by Charles to the Duke of York, and was by him immediately assigned to Lords Berkeley and Carteret with all the proprietary rights which accompanied the original grant. They took measures to induce emigration; and their concessions were so liberal that in a short time numerous flourishing towns were established by people from the other colonies and from England.

The Government. The government which the proprietors set up was to be exercised by a governor and council and general assembly. The governor was to be appointed by the proprietors, the council by the governor. The general assembly was the legislature. It was to consist of the governor and council, and deputies chosen by the freemen of the towns. This body was to make laws subject to the approval of the proprietary. It had power to constitute courts, to levy taxes, to provide for the defence of the province, and to make annual appropriations for maintaining the government. Thus the privileges for which some of the other colonies struggled for years were granted at the outset; especially the right to lay taxes, and to control the provincial expenditures. The right to appeal to the proprietor was granted in all cases. Freedom of conscience and worship was also secured. Local charters of incorporation were given to the various communities, by which they were empowered to make their own by-laws, to choose their own municipal officers, and to hold courts for deciding small causes.

These local governments went at once into operation, and continued without interruption; but the provincial government was for a long time in a confused state. The demand of the proprietors for the payment of annual quit-rents met with much opposition, especially from those who had occupied the land previous to the grant to Berkeley and Carteret. Some of the towns refused to acknowledge the jurisdiction of the proprietors; and the meetings of the general assembly were frequently suspended for several years.

Disturbed Administration.

About ten years from the establishment of the proprietary authority, the province was divided; and the western portion came into the hands of William Penn and several others, who proceeded to exercise the proprietary right of jurisdiction. A government was established, consisting of a governor and council, and an assembly representing the people. This assembly was to have the appointment of all officers except the governor, was to fix salaries, and to levy taxes. Liberty of conscience was allowed; and, in general, the principles of popular government were recognized. The province was divided into "tenths;" and these into "proprieties," each of which chose a representative. Two districts for judicial purposes were established, and courts organized. This part of the province was settled chiefly by Quakers from England and Ireland.

Division of the Province.

New Government.

East New Jersey soon after came into the hands of the same Quaker proprietors who owned the western province; but the form of government remained essentially the same. Counties were soon established in both provinces, and courts established; and the representatives to the assembly came to be chosen by the counties, instead of by the "tenths."

During the first thirty years of the history of the colony, there were continual disputes between the proprietors and the Duke of York, between the successive proprietors themselves, and between the proprietors and the people. There was hardly any time when there was not more or less confusion in the administration of public affairs. This unfortunate condition was terminated in 1702, when the proprietors surrendered to the crown all their jurisdiction in both provinces. In that year, one royal province was formed, with a governor and council appointed by the crown, and an assembly of deputies chosen partly by counties and partly by some of the towns. A large property qualification was required both for the representatives and for the voters; but this was afterward diminished. Laws made were subject to the negative of the governor, and were to be transmitted to the crown for approval. The governor and council were authorized to constitute courts of justice, and to appoint all judicial officers.

New Jersey becomes a Royal Province.

Thus it appears that the new government was much less favorable to the interests of the people than the old had been. The control of the judiciary, of expenditures, and of its own sessions, was taken from the assembly, and nothing given in their place. New Jersey, like Massachusetts, had less political liberty in the second period of its history than in the first; and it was this very change which prepared the people for complete independence. From this time until the Revolution, the history of New Jersey resembles that of the other provinces. The royal governors

Preparation for Independence.

were frequently haughty and exacting, the assemblies sometimes submissive, but more often persistent in resisting what were considered violations of their rights. The people were gradually driven to see that the only security for permanent peace was in independence; and they united readily with the other colonies in securing it.

SUMMARY.

1. The territory between the Connecticut and the Delaware Rivers was claimed by the Dutch, and called New Netherlands.

2. From 1615 to 1621, settlements were made at New York and Albany, under the Dutch West India Company.

3. Political power was wholly in the hands of a director-general and a council appointed by the company. For the first thirty years, the people had no voice either in the local or general administration.

4. The people became dissatisfied with their condition, contrasting it with the freedom of New England; but their complaints were not heeded.

5. King Charles of England gave the territory to the Duke of York, who took it from the Dutch in 1664.

6. The people obtained no voice in the colonial government until 1683, when a representative assembly was formed, and a charter of liberties granted.

7. On the accession of the Duke of York to the throne of England as James II., the colony became a royal province, and was under the government of Andros.

8. Under William and Mary, the colony came to be

governed in nearly the same manner as Massachusetts; and the people, from this time, were earnest in defence of their political privileges.

9. The territory of New Jersey was granted by the Duke of York to proprietors, who encouraged emigration, and gave to the settlers extensive political powers.

10. The local administration was in the hands of the people, and continued to be so without interruption. Dissension between the proprietors and the people caused the colonial government to be frequently in a confused state.

11. The colony next came under the control of William Penn and others, by whom the people were favorably treated; but the dissension continued.

12. In 1702 the colony became a royal province, governed like the others, and subject to the same encroachments of king and parliament.

CHAPTER XV.

THE COLONIES OF PENNSYLVANIA, DELAWARE, AND MARYLAND.

PENNSYLVANIA AND DELAWARE.

Early Settlements.

SOON after the colonization of New York by the Dutch, a company of Swedes settled on the Delaware near the present site of Newcastle; and they extended their limits northward nearly to where Philadelphia is now situated, and southward. After a few years, the Dutch governor of New Netherlands compelled them to submit to his rule; and they were governed in the same way as the villages of New York. After the conquest by the English, this whole territory was claimed by the Duke of York, and, being formed into three counties, was under the control of the English governor of New York. The laws of England were substituted for those of Holland; and Newcastle was incorporated as a city with the usual officers.

United to New York.

In 1681 William Penn obtained from Charles II. a grant of the land now included in the State of Pennsylvania. The description of the southern boundary seemed to conflict with the claims of the proprietor of Maryland; and disputes arose which were not settled until 1763. In that year,

Grants to Penn.

the final survey was made; and the boundary has since been famous as Mason and Dixon's line. This charter gave to Penn the usual proprietary right to govern the settlers, and to appoint officers, but also required him to hold assemblies of the people for legislation.

Settlements by Penn.

At the date of Penn's charter, there were within the limits of his province some Dutch and Swedes; and he soon obtained from the Duke of York a cession of the lower counties, as they were called, on the Delaware. Penn immediately sent out a colony under a deputy governor. The next year he came himself; and the country along the river was rapidly filled by Quakers from England and the Continent. No other colony grew so rapidly, nor from the beginning was so flourishing.

Government under Penn.

Penn very early divided the province into counties, from each of which delegates were chosen both to the provincial council and to the assembly. The council consisted of eighteen persons chosen by ballot by the freemen of the counties for three years, one-third retiring annually. This body, with the governor or deputy governor, who presided, had power to prepare all bills, and propose them to the assembly, together with the general executive power, the management of the finances and of schools, and the establishment of courts of justice. The governor could do nothing without the consent of this body. The assembly consisted of a large number of delegates chosen in the same manner as the councillors. Judges, sheriffs, coroners, and justices of the peace were appointed and commissioned by the governor. The proprietor made no change in the form of government without the consent of the council and assembly; but in the council he had three votes.

In 1684 Penn returned to England, leaving the administration of affairs in the hands of the provincial council. While there, dissatisfied with proceedings at home, he commissioned five members of the council to act as his deputies in transacting executive business; afterwards, a single deputy governor was appointed. About this time the territories, as they were called, — that is, the three counties on the lower Delaware, — became dissatisfied with the administration, and established a separate legislature.

Penn's Absence.

In 1692, by William and Mary, Penn's province was taken from him, and placed under the jurisdiction of the royal governor of New York; but in 1696 Penn was re-instated in his proprietary rights. His deputy, Markham, to satisfy the people, who were not quite contented with their political relations, made a new frame of government. The number of members of the council and assembly was diminished. Freemen were required to be twenty-one years of age, to have resided two years in the province, and to possess certain property. The assembly was given power to initiate legislation, submitting bills to the council for approbation. The establishment of a judiciary was in the hands of the assembly.

Change in Government.

Freemen.

Though Penn's government seems to have been, on the whole, liberal, the people were always more or less dissatisfied. On his return to the province, in 1701, he gave them a new charter of privileges, extending slightly the powers of the assembly, and also giving to the freemen the privilege of nominating to him persons for

Further Changes in the Government.

sheriffs and other inferior officers. The territories, which had been again united to Pennsylvania, were given permission to have a separate legislature, which they availed themselves of; and they remained separate to this extent until the Revolution, but having the same proprietary governor. By this new charter, the powers of the council were withdrawn, and the governor acted alone. All forms of religion were tolerated. After the death of Penn, his sons inherited his proprietary rights, and appointed deputy governors to administer the government. There was a council named by the proprietors, but not forming a branch of the legislature as formerly. The judges were appointed by the deputy governor; but all salaries were granted by the assembly, which managed the revenues, and had exclusive control over its own sessions. Sheriffs and coroners were chosen by the people, and also such local officers as assessors, overseers of the poor, and pound-keepers. The township system was not so complete as in New England; but the principle of local self-government was recognized and acted upon. Thus in Pennsylvania and Delaware there had been a gain in the extent of their political privileges; and they continued in this comparatively independent condition until the Revolution.

MARYLAND.

The colonial history of Maryland is especially interesting because it presents the first proprietary government, the first royal charter granting to the colonists a voice in legislation, and the first example of complete religious toleration. Its territory was granted by Charles I. to Lord Baltimore, a Roman Catholic nobleman, with full proprietary rights (1632). He might make laws with the advice, consent, and approbation of the freemen of the province; but the laws must not be repugnant to the laws of England. He might impose taxes for his own benefit; and the king agreed that no tax should ever be laid upon the colony by royal authority. He might establish tribunals, erect churches, and control ecclesiastical affairs. He might appoint provincial officers, repel invasions, and suppress insurrections. All these powers were to be hereditary in the family of the proprietor. It is a striking feature of the times, illustrating the feudal ideas that still prevailed, that the king without consulting parliament could convey to a subject such almost kingly powers.

Proprietary Charter.

In 1634 the first settlement was made by a company of Catholics, mostly men of means. The next year the first colonial assembly met, consisting of all the freemen of the province. There is no record of their proceedings. As the colony increased, a necessity for legislation arose; and the proprietor framed a code of laws, which he sent to the governor to propose to the freemen. A second assembly was called; and, though no fault was found with the laws, the colonists refused to allow the initiative of the proprietor, and would not ratify the code. They drew up a code of their own; but this was never ratified.

Colonial Assemblies.

In 1639 a third assembly was called; and at this time the representative system was established. The governor might personally summon such persons as he chose; and the people might send as many delegates as the freemen should think proper. A peculiar provision allowed any free-

Representative System Established.

man who had not voted for a deputy to have a seat himself in the legislature. The assembly thus consisted of the governor, secretary, those specially called, and the representatives, called burgesses. These were elected from counties. All sat and voted as one body until 1649; when it was enacted that the persons called by the proprietor should form an upper house, and those elected by the colonists a lower house, each having a negative upon the other.

Judiciary. The assembly of 1639 established a judiciary system, and made such laws as were necessary. In civil cases the governor was made sole judge. Capital crimes were to be tried by a jury before the governor and his council. County courts were also established. The assembly remained the final court of appeal. The people early affirmed the principle that no taxes should be imposed without the consent of the assembly; but they continued to maintain the most grateful and friendly relations to the proprietor.

Religious Toleration. The most remarkable enactment was that which established religious freedom: "No person within this province professing to believe in Jesus Christ shall be in any ways troubled, molested, or discountenanced for his or her religion, or in the free exercise thereof." The only other colony which at this time professed toleration was Rhode Island; and there Catholics were excepted. The colony grew quite rapidly; but the new-comers were mostly Protestants. During the rule of Cromwell and the Puritan party in England, the Protestants acquired the supremacy in the provincial assembly, and proceeded to disfranchise the Catholic settlers; but toleration was afterward re-established.

The general features of the government underwent no important change until the Revolution. Unlike the more northern colonies, the people were unwilling to gather in towns; and, in consequence, churches were few and poorly sustained, and little opportunity was afforded for education.

The Royal Government.

The religion of the proprietor subjected him to constant misrepresentation and injustice; and the peace of the colony was frequently disturbed by quarrels growing out of religious differences. During the reign of William and Mary, the proprietor's political rights were withdrawn, and a royal governor was appointed. The province was divided into parishes, in each of which a Protestant minister was to be appointed by the governor, and supported by a tax upon all the inhabitants. The Church of England was set up, and Catholics were persecuted. In the parishes, the management of affairs was placed in the hands of vestries elected by the Protestant inhabitants: and free schools and libraries were by law established in all the parishes; but these were not flourishing. Such local matters as in New England devolved upon the selectmen were in Maryland cared for by the parochial officers. But these soon ceased to be elective, and not only held their office for life, but filled the vacancies in their bodies by their own appointment. After a suspension of the rights of the proprietors for twenty-four years, they were restored to a descendant of Lord Baltimore who was a Protestant.

SUMMARY.

1. The territory of Delaware was settled by Swedes and Dutch, afterward came into the hands of the Duke of York, and was by him ceded to William Penn.

2. Pennsylvania was granted to Penn by Charles II., and was settled by English Quakers in 1681.

3. The first government established by Penn gave to the people the choice of a legislative assembly and an executive council. The local officers were appointed by the proprietor.

4. Subsequent changes were made in the government, all increasing the political privileges of the people.

5. After the death of Penn, his son inherited his proprietary rights, and exercised his authority through a deputy. The people now, in their assembly, had complete legislative power, and controlled their own sessions and the finances of the colony. They also controlled the local administration.

6. The Delaware counties obtained a separate legislature, but had the same executive as Pennsylvania. Both remained under the proprietor until the Revolution.

7. Maryland was settled by English Catholics under Lord Baltimore, who received proprietary power from Charles I.

8. In the charter, the king forever exempted the colonists from taxation by royal authority.

9. The people were represented in a legislative assembly, and early insisted upon making their own laws, subject to the approval of the proprietor or his deputy.

10. The proprietor established religious toleration, trial by jury, and local courts of justice; and the people claimed exemption from taxes levied without their consent.

11. During the reign of William and Mary, the Church of England was established. The colony was

divided into parishes each with a Protestant minister supported by general tax. The management of local affairs came into the hands of parish officers who held their place for life. There were no towns.

12. The colony remained proprietary until the Revolution.

CHAPTER XVI.

THE SOUTHERN COLONIES.

VIRGINIA.

The London Company.

THE early political history of Virginia is the history of the London Company, whose formation we have already noticed. This company, to which was given the power to transport settlers, and found colonies, was placed under the control of a council resident in England, the members of which were appointed by the king. Local affairs in the colony were to be managed by an inferior council resident in the colony, the members likewise appointed by the king. Power was afterwards given to this council to elect a president, to remove members, and to fill vacancies in its membership. Judicial power was placed in the hands of the president and council; and they also had such legislative functions as the king did not himself exercise. The settlers had no political rights whatever. Property was to be held in common for five years. Under this charter, Virginia received the first permanent English colony (1607).

The Colony.

The object of the company was solely commercial profit; and the settlers had no higher motive. They came without families, and with no intention of making the New World a permanent residence. Community of property, even when all the members of society are well disposed, is fatal to progress; but when a large proportion are idle and vicious nothing but disaster can follow. The colony suffered from scarcity of food, from disease, from the Indians, and from the rivalries and jealousies of those who had been appointed to the council.

New Charter.

In two years, the company received a new charter, which enlarged its own powers without increasing the liberty of the colonists. The local council, with its president, was abolished. A single council in England was empowered to manage all colonial affairs, to make laws, and to provide for their execution. The king had less power than before; but the colony had no more. Under this charter, governors were appointed, who administered a military code of laws prepared in England, making such additions to it as they pleased. This absolute power, in the hands of wise and well-meaning men, promoted the prosperity of the colony; but it gave to unprincipled men opportunity for the greatest injustice.

The Colonial Assembly.

The company in England changed from an aristocratic to a democratic body, the council being abolished, and all business transacted in general meetings. This change proved favorable to the political interests of the colony; and, in 1619, a governor was appointed, limited in his executive authority by a council also appointed by the company. He found existing seven distinct plantations, to which he added four more, composed of new settlers. In each of these was a commandant, who was chief of the militia, and civil magistrate.

From each of these plantations, were summoned two representatives, called burgesses; and these, with the governor and council, constituted the first colonial legislature in America.

The Constitution. The company, in 1621, gave to the colony a written constitution. This provided that all laws made by the assembly, to be valid, should be ratified by the company, and that the regulations of the company should also be submitted to the assembly. Trial by jury was also established. The governor and council acted as a court of law; but appeals might be made to the assembly, and from that body to the company. The established religion had been from the first that of the Church of England. Now the plantations were divided into parishes, in each of which a clergyman was to be maintained by a general tax.

Legislation. During the next few years, the first extant laws of Virginia were enacted. In every plantation there was to be a church and a burial-ground. Absence from public worship was prohibited. No taxes were to be levied by the governor without the consent of the assembly; and the same limitation was made to the expenditure of public money. Thus early did Virginia declare the great principles of political liberty.

Local Government. In every parish, three men were to be sworn to see that each settler planted and tended corn enough for his family. Each parish was also to have a granary, to which every settler was annually to bring a certain amount of corn. This was to be distributed by vote of a majority of the freemen of the parish. This curious provision against scarcity is especially important as showing how early the idea of intrusting the management of purely local affairs to the people of the district gained a foothold, and found an expression.

In 1624 the company charter was taken away, and the government of the colony came into the hands of the king; but there was no change in the form of the government. In 1632 a new code of laws was made, which resembled in many respects those more stringent enactments for which New England has been celebrated. Attendance at church and orderly behavior there, temperance, and purity were enjoined; and persons might be fined for not catechising their children and ignorant persons under their charge. The voters in the parish received power to lay out highways. The election of judicial and executive officers seems to have been in the hands of the governor and council.

Becomes a Royal Province.

In 1643 some important changes were made. Counties were established, and courts set up to be held six times a year by commissioners appointed by the assembly. Parish vestries were required to be organized, the vestrymen to be chosen by the parishioners. Soon after this, a new and permanent provision was made, requiring that the voters in each county should assemble at a place named by the sheriff, and give their votes *viva voce* for two representatives in the house of burgesses. This was an imitation of the English election custom.

Formation of Counties.

For a few years, during the time of the Commonwealth, the assembly elected the governor and council, and Virginia was independent; but, after the Restoration, the king resumed his authority. Up to this time, the political institutions of

Growth of an Aristocracy.

Virginia had been nearly as free as those of the northern colonies; but now a change took place. The settlers had scattered over a large territory; and the few landholders were cultivating extensive tracts by means of slaves and white persons bound to service. These persons came now to have all political power. The parish vestries were to fill their own vacancies; the county courts were to be held by eight justices of the peace appointed by the governor; and these county courts were to levy the county taxes, make the county by-laws, and appoint the surveyors of the highways. Thus the local administration, which, in New England, was in the hands of the town officers chosen by the people, was vested in county officers appointed by the governor. Still later than this, a law was made, that none but householders and freeholders should have a voice in the election of burgesses.

The practical working of the system is described in a book written at the time. "On each of the great rivers of the province are men, in number from ten to thirty, who by trade and industry have got very competent estates. These gentlemen take care to supply the poorer sort with goods and necessaries, and are sure to keep them always in their debt, and consequently dependent on them. Out of this number, are chosen the council, assembly, justices, and other officers of government." It is said that the same causes which tended in Virginia to build up a local aristocracy operated also in Maryland.

There was no essential change in the form or principle of government until the Revolution. There were frequent disputes between the royal governors and the assemblies about their respective powers, just as there were in all the provinces. Virginia was one of the foremost in resisting the oppressive commercial measures of the English government; and the resolution of independence was presented by her delegates in the Continental Congress.

NORTH AND SOUTH CAROLINA.

Proprietors. These two colonies had so much in common, that a description of the political features of either is a description of both. The territory occupied by both was included in a grant made by Charles II. to eight noblemen (1663) in a proprietary charter copied from that given to Lord Baltimore.

Settlements. A few refugees from Virginia had occupied the soil about the Chowan River; and some planters from Barbadoes settled at the mouth of the Cape Fear. To each of these companies, the proprietor gave the privilege of nominating a certain number of persons from whom a governor and council should be selected. These, with an assembly chosen by the people, should form the government. Another settlement was made near the present site of Charleston (1670). This was governed in a similar manner. After a time the Cape Fear settlement united with that at Charleston.

The Grand Model. The proprietors had prepared a constitution which embodied the worst features of monarchical and feudal government. It was so complicated, and so unsuited to the character and circumstances of the people, that it was never put into execution, though some attempts were made. The early history is full of disputes between the colonies and the agents of the proprietors, most of whom used their position for mercenary ends. After about twenty years, the Grand Model, as it was called, was set aside; but the government went on as before. Each of the proprietors had a delegate in the council in each province.

Religion.

The colonists were of various nationalities and sects; and considerable trouble arose concerning religion. The proprietors wished to establish the Church of England, but there were large numbers of dissenters of different names. Sometimes these were allowed equal privileges with the others; but ultimately Episcopacy was established, and was supported by law until the Revolution.

Elections.

In 1705 the colony was divided into parishes. Until 1716, the members of the assembly of South Carolina had been chosen by such of the freemen as chose to assemble at Charleston for the purpose; but in this year the parishes were made election districts. About the same time, the northern province was also divided into parishes with the usual officers.

Royal Governments.

In 1720 the people rebelled against the proprietary government, and a royal governor was sent to Charleston; and in 1729 the whole province was purchased by the crown, and separate royal governors were appointed for the two colonies. From this time, the government resembled that of other royal provinces. It is impossible to present a picture of the early political life of either of these colonies. There are no records of the mode in which the assemblies were chosen or organized; and nothing is known as to the qualifications required for suffrage. There was never so large a number of indentured white persons as in Virginia; and consequently there was not so wide a difference in social and political rank as in that State.

The people were so scattered that churches and schools could not be maintained; and there was less local political activity than in the more densely populated colonies.

GEORGIA.

Grant to Trustees.

Georgia was not only settled last of the thirteen colonies, but it differed from them all in its early civil relations. A number of philanthropic gentlemen received from the king a charter, vesting in them as trustees, for twenty-one years, the territory between the Savannah and Altamaha Rivers (1732). Their object was, to provide a home for those unfortunate persons whom failure in trade and other causes had brought to poverty, and upon whom the laws of England pressed with most unjust severity.

Administration.

The trustees were to grant small portions of land to settlers of this class whom they should induce to emigrate. There were to be no large estates, and no slavery was to be tolerated. The trustees received the whole power of legislation. The affairs of the corporation were to be in the hands of a council; and such officers as were necessary were to be appointed for the colony by this council. Beside the English poor, the colony was increased by German Protestants, by Scotch Highlanders, and by Moravians. The government by the council having proved unsatisfactory, a single executive officer was appointed, styled president, acting with whom were four councillors.

Royal Government.

After about twenty years, a colonial assembly was called, not to legislate, but to advise. In 1751 the trustees surrendered their charter to the crown; and a provincial government of the usual form was at once established, and continued until the Revolution.

SUMMARY.

1. Virginia was settled under the direction of the London Company.

2. At first the king controlled the affairs of the company, and the colonists were wholly without political privileges.

3. In 1621 the colony received a written constitution establishing a representative assembly. The consent of this body was required to make any law of the company valid. Trial by jury was also established.

4. The assembly early declared that no tax could be levied without its consent, and assumed the right to control the expenditure of the public money.

5. In 1624 the colony became a royal province, and continued so until the Revolution.

6. Local administration early came to be intrusted to parish officers: afterward it was vested in county officers appointed by the governor.

7. Political power came to be chiefly in the hands of the wealthy landholders.

8. The territory of the Carolinas was granted by Charles II. to eight English noblemen.

9. The colonists were few and widely scattered, and could not be governed by the complicated constitution made by the proprietors. In each colony the proprietors were represented by a governor, and the people by an assembly.

10. The colony finally became a royal province, governed like the others.

11. The people always guarded their liberty jealous-

ly, and resisted all attempts of the proprietors to tax them.

12. Georgia was founded as a refuge for the poor of England. The land, at first, was held by trustees, who governed the people arbitrarily.

13. Afterward a better class of settlers came; the king assumed control; and the colony was governed like the other royal provinces.

CHAPTER XVII.

DECLARATION OF INDEPENDENCE.

From the beginning of colonial history, as we have seen, there had been disputes between the home government and the colonies concerning their respective authority. At first Massachusetts had been the chief defender of colonial claims; but after the revolution of 1689 had settled political affairs in England, and both parties united in a general colonial policy, all the colonies were strenuous in asserting their rights.

Claims of the Colonies.

During all their history, the colonists acknowledged themselves subjects of England, and successively proclaimed the Commonwealth and the sovereigns who followed it. They admitted the authority of Parliament in general legislation, and adopted the English statutes and the common law as far as their local circumstances made it possible to do so. They were willing to defend the person and territory of their sovereign against foreign enemies to the extent of their means.

On the other hand, they claimed, that, in emigrating to America, they had not forfeited any of the rights of English subjects. Foremost of these were those conferred by Magna Charta, trial by jury, and the writ of *habeas corpus*. Beside these, they claimed the right of making their own laws, not repugnant to laws of England, through their representatives freely chosen; and especially they insisted, as Englishmen, that no tax should be imposed upon them but such as they freely voted in their local assemblies. Massachusetts, through all her early history, claimed the right of ultimate judicial decision in all cases whatsoever, and denied the legality of appeal to any English authority.

English View of American Claims.

The sovereigns of the Stuart family, who had little respect for the rights of Englishmen at home, could hardly be expected to treat these claims of their American subjects with much more consideration. They had some pretext for their arbitrary measures in the complaints and petitions that were continually urged upon their notice. The restrictive policy of the Massachusetts colonies made them many enemies. The friends of Episcopacy complained that the acts of supremacy and uniformity were set at naught; Baptists and Quakers, that they were persecuted and banished; Mason and Gorges, that their authority had been usurped, and their chartered rights infringed; Rhode Island, that Massachusetts was grasping and bigoted; and the London merchants, that the navigation acts were openly violated. All united in the assertion that the people of Massachusetts Bay were disloyal, and only waiting a favorable opportunity to dissolve their allegiance, and set up for themselves. In consequence of these calumnies, Massachusetts lost her original charter; but her misfortune was soon shared by all the northern colonies. When, under James II., popular government ceased to exist in England, all colonial rights were suspended.

Soon after the accession of William and Mary, a more

definite policy was adopted. Previous to this time, the control of American affairs had been in the hands of the privy council of the king, or of commissioners appointed by that body. About 1700 Parliament took control of the administration of the colonies, and began a series of restrictive measures designed to cripple colonial industry, and increase the dependence of the provinces upon the mother country.

Restrictive Colonial Policy.

The navigation acts had always been a source of trouble between the two countries. In 1651 the Long Parliament, aiming a blow at Dutch commerce, enacted that no goods should be imported into England but in English ships, or in ships belonging to the nation where the goods were produced. This statute was not enforced against the colonists. The first parliament after the Restoration re-enacted this law with most important additions. It was ordered that no merchandise should be imported into the colonies but in English vessels navigated by Englishmen. Such American products as would not compete with those of England were forbidden to be exported to any but English ports. Sugar, tobacco, ginger, indigo, cotton, and dyewoods were included in this class. Other articles which might also be produced in England could only be sold in ports south of Cape Finisterre. Soon another law required that all European commodities imported into the colonies should be in English ships from England. The colonists were thus compelled to buy and sell in England, in order to build up the interests of English merchants. Officers were stationed in the colonial ports to enforce these regulations. The first attempt to cripple the

Navigation Acts.

manufacturing interest of the colonies was by a statute of William IH., forbidding the exportation of wool and woollen goods out of the colonies, or from one colony to another. Next the manufacture of hats was forbidden; and in 1733 a heavy duty was imposed upon the products of the West Indies imported into the colonies. Meanwhile the royal governors were in frequent collision with the colonial assemblies. In Massachusetts, there were long disputes about salary. The General Court insisted upon voting the governor's allowance annually, and regulated its amount by his disposition towards them. In New York, freedom of the press was the principal question at issue.

Declaratory Resolves.

In 1764 the celebrated Declaratory Resolves were presented in the House of Commons. These resolutions announced the intention of the government to raise a revenue in the colonies by a stamp tax. This met with the most strenuous opposition from the colonists; and when, in the next year, the Act passed, it occasioned the first open resistance. The story of the next ten years is too familiar to be repeated here. The opposition of the colonies only served to strengthen the determination of the British government; and, as the scheme of taxation became more and more fully developed, the purpose of the colonists to resist acquired definiteness, and became nearly universal.

Progress of Independence.

When the coercive measures of the goverment forced the colonists into the war of the Revolution, the royal officers were obliged to withdraw. This necessitated temporary arrangements; and in all the colonies provisional governments were established. During the year 1775, while the country was everywhere preparing to resist the forces of the British government, the thought of independence was not tolerated. To defend their rights until reconciliation could be effected, and arbitrary measures repealed, was the only purpose of the mass of the colonists. But when all their petitions had been disregarded, or treated with contempt; when the king had publicly proclaimed them rebels, had said in private, "I am unalterably determined at every hazard, at the risk of every consequence, to compel the colonies to absolute submission," and when he had hired German troops to carry out this purpose, — the tone of public sentiment changed; and throughout the country the one subject of thought was independence.

First Steps.

Several months elapsed before the minds of the people were fully prepared for the important step; and at the last moment there was a strong party which thought the time had not come. Meantime, one by one, the several colonial assemblies gave their voice for independence. Bancroft says, "Comprehensive instructions reaching independence, though not using the word, had been given by Massachusetts in January; by South Carolina in March; by Georgia, April 5; North Carolina on the fourteenth of April expressly declared in favor of independence; Rhode Island, May 14; Virginia, May 15; Connecticut, June 14; New Hampshire, June 15; New York, June 21; Pennsylvania, June 28; Delaware, June 15. In May the assembly of Virginia instructed her delegates in Congress to propose a declaration of independence; and accordingly, on the seventh of June, Richard Henry Lee proposed the following resolution: "That these United Colonies are and of right ought to be free and independent states, that they are absolved from all allegiance to the British crown, and that all political connection between them and the state of Great Britain is and ought to be totally dissolved." This resolution was discussed on the eighth, postponed until the eleventh, and then postponed three weeks, and a committee was appointed to prepare a formal declaration meantime.

Resolution Proposed.

On the first of July, the resolution came before Congress again for discussion. The vote was taken on the next day, and twelve colonies voted in favor. New York did not vote. On the two succeeding days, Congress discussed the draft of a declaration which Jefferson had written for the committee, and on the fourth it was adopted by twelve States.

Resolution Adopted.

(For copy of Declaration see Appendix.)

PART III.

THE CONSTITUTIONAL GOVERNMENT OF MASSACHUSETTS.

CHAPTER XVIII.

FORMATION OF THE CONSTITUTION. — THE LEGISLATIVE DEPARTMENT.

FORMATION OF CONSTITUTION.

DURING all the troubles between the colonies and the home government, Massachusetts had been especially prominent. She thus brought upon herself the earliest and most severe coercive measures of the crown. Her commerce was destroyed by the famous Port Bill; and British troops were sent to awe her people.

Regulating Act.

When these measures failed to stifle the spirit of independence, the king in 1774 procured the passage of what is known as the Regulating Act; which not only essentially changed the form of government established by the charter, but struck a heavy blow at some of the fundamental safeguards of civil liberty. This act vested the appointment of councillors in the king, and of all judicial officers in the governor. The governor and council were empowered to appoint sheriffs, by whom jurymen were to be selected. Town meetings were forbidden to be held without the consent of the governor. At the same time, another law provided that persons might be transported to England for trial. It was found impossible to carry these measures into execution. No persons could be found to serve as jurymen; and the administration of justice was suspended. Gradually the people were being driven into independence. The colony asked the advice of the Continental Congress, and were counselled to avoid hasty measures, and to be guided by events.

Provincial Congress.

In October, 1774, the governor had called for an election of deputies, but had dissolved the court before the time of meeting. The body met, notwithstanding, in Salem, and organized itself into a provincial congress with John Hancock as president. This body took into consideration the affairs of the province, and appointed an executive committee called "The Committee of Safety."

Provisional Government.

After the battle of Lexington, Massachusetts again called upon the Continental Congress for advice. The people of the country were not ready for independence; and the Congress was unwilling to advise Massachusetts to set up a new government. It therefore recommended that the people choose representatives according to the terms of their charter, who should choose a council to govern the State until a royal governor might be appointed who should carry out the provisions of the charter. Such a governor never appeared; and the council administered the affairs until 1780.

Adoption of Constitution.

In that year, a convention of delegates, chosen by the people, prepared a constitution, which was ratified by a popular vote. In October, 1780, the new constitutional State government was organized, with John Hancock as governor. The State has since been governed under this constitution with such amendments as have from time to time been made to it.

The constitution is preceded by a preamble, which states the object of government, and the nature and duties of the body politic. It declares that government is *for* the people, and should therefore be *by* the people. This preamble is followed by a very complete declaration of rights. Starting with the assertion that "all men are born free and equal," it declares the right of self-government; the accountability of officers to the people; the right to freedom in electing and being elected; the right of personal protection; freedom from taxation without consent of people; the right to free, complete, and prompt justice; to trial by jury, and in the vicinity where the subject events happen; to security from unreasonable search and seizure of person and papers; liberty of the press; liberty to keep and bear arms for the common defence; subordination of military to civil authority; the right of the people peaceably to assemble, and to petition the legislature; freedom of speech in the legislature; freedom from excessive bail and fines, and from cruel and unusual punishments; exemption from quartering soldiers, and from martial law. It is also declared that judges should hold office during good behavior, and that the departments of government should be distinct, "to the end it may be a government of laws, and not of men."

Preamble.

Bill of Rights.

It will be observed that these rights are the same that had been asserted by Magna Charta, by the Petition of Right, and by the Bill of Rights signed by William and Mary. They had been contended for by Englishmen during six hundred years, and by the American colonists for a century and a half.

The second part of the constitution treats of the

frame of government. It declares the name of the body politic to be the Commonwealth of Massachusetts.

THE LEGISLATIVE DEPARTMENT.

General Court and its Branches. The legislative department retains the name by which it has been known from the days of the company charter. It is still called the General Court, and consists of a Senate and House of Representatives. It is invested with full powers to constitute courts of justice, to enact laws, to provide for the election and appointment of officers whose election is not provided for in the constitution, and to prescribe their duties, and to levy taxes.

Powers.

Senate, Members of. The Senate consists of forty members. Each member must have been an inhabitant of the Commonwealth for five years, at least, immediately preceding his election, and at the time of his election must be an inhabitant of the district for which he is chosen. If he cease to be an inhabitant of the State, he ceases to be a senator.

Districts. In every tenth year from 1865, a census is taken of the inhabitants and voters in each city and town in the State. The General Court, at its first session after the census, divides the State into forty districts of adjacent territory in such a way that they contain as nearly as possible an equal number of voters, yet without dividing a town, or ward of a city, and generally without uniting parts of two counties in one district. Each district elects one senator.

Vacancies. A vacancy in the senate is filled by election by the people of the district, upon the order of a majority of the senators elected.

A quorum for doing business consists of a majority of the members, though a less number may organize temporarily, adjourn from day to day, and compel the attendance of absent members.

Quorum.

The house of representatives consists of two hundred and forty members. Each must have been an inhabitant of the district which he represents for at least one year next preceding his election, and ceases to represent the district if he ceases to be an inhabitant of the Commonwealth.

House of Representatives. Members of.

At the first session of the legislature after the census, the representatives are apportioned to the counties according to the number of voters in each. Then the county commissioners, or a special board chosen for the purpose, divide the county into districts, without dividing any town, or ward of a city. These districts elect a number of representatives according to the number of voters they contain; but no district elects more than three. Thus the number of districts is not the same as the number of representatives.

Districts.

When a vacancy occurs in the representation of any district, the Speaker of the house orders a new election by the people at a specified time.

Vacancies.

A quorum consists of a majority of members; but a less number may meet as in the senate.

Quorum.

Each house is the final judge of the election and qualification of its own members: that is, if a question arises between two or more persons as to which is legally elected to either house, the members of that house, after proper investi-

Privileges of each House.

gation, decide between them; and this decision is final.

Each house chooses its own officers, and establishes its own rules of proceeding. It may also punish, by imprisonment not exceeding thirty days, any person, not a member, who is guilty of disrespect to the house by disorderly conduct, or by refusing to testify before its committees.

Each house may adjourn for a period not exceeding two days.

The members of the houses are free from arrest on civil process while going to, returning from, and attending sessions of the court.

Money Bills.

The house of representatives originates all money bills; but the senate may propose or concur in amendments as on other bills. This provision was copied from the English constitution, which gives to the house of commons the exclusive right to legislate respecting revenue. The house of lords may not even amend. Money bills are those which provide for raising money by taxation, or for expending it for the usual purposes or in special cases.

Organization of House of Representatives.

The Constitution provides that the General Court shall assemble every year on the first Wednesday of January. (Previous to that time, certificates have been given to the members elected, and duplicates sent to the secretary of the Commonwealth.) Between ten and twelve o'clock on the appointed day, the members elect of the house gather in the representatives' hall, and are called to order by the eldest

Calling to Order.

senior member present, who presides until a speaker is chosen. By the eldest senior member is meant the person whose membership dates farthest back. Thus in the legislature of 1875, if there is a person who was a member in 1845, and no one who was a member before that date, he calls the house to order. The certificates are then collected and examined; and, if a quorum is found to be present, the governor is notified of the fact, and that the members are ready to be qualified; that is, to take the required oaths.

Oaths.

The governor with his council then appears, and administers the following oaths to each member:—

The Oath of Allegiance.—"I —— —— do solemnly swear that I will bear true faith and allegiance to the Commonwealth of Massachusetts, and will support the constitution thereof. So help me God."

The Oath of Office.—"I —— —— do solemnly swear and affirm that I will faithfully and impartially discharge and perform all the duties incumbent on me as representative, according to the best of my abilities and understanding, agreeably to the rules and regulations of the Constitution, and laws of this Commonwealth. So help me God."

The Oath of Allegiance to the United States.—"I —— —— do solemnly swear that I will support the Constitution of the United States. So help me God."

Each member takes and subscribes the foregoing oaths. Some members, having conscientious scruples against oaths, make affirmation to the same pledges.

Officers.

After being duly qualified, the members of the house proceed to choose by ballot one of their number as a presiding officer, called the Speaker. This name is borrowed from the British Parliament. They next choose by ballot a clerk, who is not a member, and whose duties are, to keep the journal of the house, to prepare a calendar of all matters in order for consideration by the house, and to read all bills and communications that may come before the house for its action. Having gone so far, notice is sent to the governor and to the senate that the house has organized, and is ready for business. On the same day, or soon, a chaplain is chosen, who opens the daily session with prayer.

The senate organizes in a similar way in its own chamber, the members being duly qualified as in the house. Its presiding officer is called the President. The two houses then choose a sergeant-at-arms, whose duties are, to execute all orders of either house; to preserve order, and prevent interruption of the business of the houses; to have general charge of the State House, superintending repairs, and seeing that all parts of it are in proper order for the use of the government; to appoint and oversee watchmen and firemen in the State House; and to appoint doorkeepers and messengers to each house of legislation.

Committees.

At the beginning of the annual session, the presiding officer of each body appoints certain standing committees, whose work it is to consider the matter presented to either house, and report what action is proper. Beside these, there is a large number of what are called joint standing committees, composed of members from both branches. There are committees upon banks, education, insurance, street railways, railroads, towns, and many other subjects. Frequently a special committee is appointed to consider a matter of temporary interest.

Mode of Making Laws.

We shall next notice how laws are made. The Constitution requires three things to be done to make a law. A measure must receive a majority vote in each branch of the legislature, and be approved by the governor. If he objects, he may return the bill with his objections to the house in which it originated. This house must enter his objections in full upon its records, and proceed to reconsider the bill. If two-thirds of this branch vote for the measure, it is sent to the other house; and, if this also assent by a two-thirds vote, the measure becomes a law without the approval of the governor. If he does not return the bill within five days, it becomes a law, unless the legislature prevent his returning it by adjourning. This power of the governor to withhold his approval from any measure is termed the veto[1] power. As he cannot really prevent a bill from becoming a law, the veto is said to be not *absolute*, but *qualified*. The governor's veto, however, has great weight and it rarely happens that a bill is enacted against his objection.

The Veto Power.

When the General Court begins its session, subjects for legislation are presented to it in three ways. The governor, in an address to the two branches, describes the condition of public affairs, and points out in what directions legislative action is necessary or desirable. Messages from the governor are referred to appropriate committees which may report thereon by bill, or otherwise. A second mode of introducing business is for an individual member to present a resolve or a bill, or an order, which he may do at any time with the consent of the house. A large part of

Introduction of Business.

[1] *Veto*, Latin, I forbid. This was the word by which the Roman tribunes refused their assent to a law which they disapproved. It was an absolute prohibition.

the business comes before the legislature in the form of petitions from the people. Thus a number of persons ask permission to establish a savings bank, a town asks leave to change its name, a man wishes to use a certain water-privilege. These petitions are generally presented through a member of the legislature, and the petition is ordinarily accompanied by a bill, embodying the legislation prayed for.

Mode of Proceeding.

To save the time of the house, all these matters, in their crude form, are referred to the appropriate committees, to be by them considered and reported on, either favorably or otherwise, as they think best. Thus the representative from the town of Greenland presents a petition to the General Court, signed by a part of his townsmen, praying that the name of the town may be changed to Sahara. The petition is at once referred to the joint standing committee on towns. This body gives public notice, that, at a certain time and place, it will hear all parties interested in the matter. After listening to the petitioners, opportunity is given to any person to remonstrate; and then the committee decides whether the change is desirable. If a majority decide in the affirmative, a bill is reported, which begins, "Be it enacted by the Senate and House of Representatives in General Court assembled, and by the authority of the same," and declares that the name of the town of Greenland shall, after a certain date, be changed to Sahara.

If the committee is opposed to the bill referred to it, it reports that the petitioners have leave to withdraw, or that the bill ought not to pass. The adverse report of the committee is not conclusive, as the house may substitute the bill for the unfavorable report, and, in that case, the bill is dealt with as if originally reported by a committee. If a bill or resolve involving an expenditure of public money or a grant of public property is reported by a committee, it is referred to another committee, called "the Committee on Ways and Means." This committee considers the financial features of the bill, and reports in its turn. In this way such measures are subjected to a double scrutiny.

The rules of each house provide that every bill shall have three separate readings, no two of which shall be on the same day.[1] The bill being reported by a committee, if no objection is made, it goes into the orders of the next day, unless some other time is specially assigned for its consideration. When it is reached in course, the title is read, each member being provided with a printed copy of the bill. This is its second reading; and the question for the house to decide is, whether it shall have a third reading. At this time, the discussion occurs on the merits of the bill; and amendments may be proposed, which may be acted on at once, or may be sent to the committee to be considered by them. If a majority vote in favor of ordering a third reading, the bill goes to a committee on such bills, whose business is to see that the bills are correctly drawn. When the bill is reported back by this committee, the house is called to vote on ordering the bill to be engrossed. This is also a debatable stage in the progress of the bill. If this vote is in the affirmative, the bill is sent to the other house, where it goes through a similar process. If it is ordered to be engrossed by this house also, it is given to an engrossing

[1] This rule is sometimes suspended so that a bill may pass through two or more stages on the same day.

clerk, who copies it in a fair, round hand, on parchment. After examination by a committee, if found to be correctly engrossed, it is enacted by the house of representatives, and then by the senate.

The details of the proceeding are regulated by the rules of each house, and by the general principles of parliamentary law.[1] If the second house amend the bill, it goes back to the house in which it originated, where a vote is taken on concurring in the amendment. If the two houses cannot agree on amendments, a committee of conference may be appointed, which endeavors to make the measure satisfactory to both parties. After a bill has passed both houses, the clerk of the senate lays it before the governor for his approbation, which he expresses by his signature.

Publication of Laws.

After each session of the General Court, the secretary of the Commonwealth causes all the acts and resolves[2] which have become laws to be bound and preserved. He also causes to be printed copies of the general laws and resolves, and distributes through the towns a sufficient number to furnish one copy to each family or eight inhabitants.

Revision of Statutes.

From time to time, the laws of the State are revised by a board appointed for the purpose. The whole body of laws, as they present it, is then enacted by the General Court like any bill, and

[1] *Parliamentary Law* comprises those general rules which regulate the conduct of business in legislative assemblies, and in all meetings for deliberative action.

[2] The Province Charter of 1691 required that all acts of the General Court should be sent to England for the approval of the king. To avoid this inconvenience, the legislature frequently passed measures in the form of *resolves*, which were not subject to the same requirement. The practice has been continued, though now resolves are subject to the same rules as other bills.

published for distribution. Such revisions have been made in 1836, 1860, 1882, and 1901. The latest revision and the annual volumes subsequently printed contain the general laws of the Commonwealth in force at any time. Such special acts as apply only to individuals or corporations are not included in the revision, but are published separately.

Amending the Constitution.

Beside the ordinary legislation, the General Court has the initiative in changing the constitution of the Commonwealth. An amendment to the constitution is introduced into the legislature and referred to a committee like any other bill. In order that any article may become valid as a part of the constitution, it must be proposed by the General Court, and agreed to by a majority of the senators, and two-thirds of the representatives present and voting. It must then be entered on the journals of the two houses, with the yeas and nays, then referred to the next General Court, and published. The same proportion of the members of the next General Court must agree to it; and then it must be submitted to the people, and be approved by a majority of the legal voters at meetings called for the purpose in the various cities and towns. Thirty-six articles of amendment have been ratified by the people.

CHAPTER XIX.

THE EXECUTIVE DEPARTMENT.

THE GOVERNOR.

THE supreme executive power is vested in a magistrate called the Governor of the Commonwealth of Massachusetts; and his title is His Excellency. He is chosen annually by the legal voters of the State. He must have been an inhabitant of the Commonwealth for seven years next preceding his election.

Induction into Office.

On the first Wednesday of January, the secretary of the Commonwealth lays before the Senate and House of Representatives the returns of election that have been sent from the several towns and cities. These bodies examine them, and declare who is elected governor. After the organization of the houses is complete, they meet in convention in the representatives' hall. The president of the senate occupies the chair, and administers to the governor elect the three oaths required by the constitution, the same that are taken by the members of the General Court. After being thus qualified, the governor delivers an address, as has been before stated.

Powers of Governor: 1. To hold Council.

The governor has authority to call together the council at his discretion, and is required to hold meetings of the council from time to time as the interests of the Commonwealth demand.

The governor has certain powers respecting sessions of the General Court, which he exercises with advice of the council. 1. If the court is in session, and the two houses desire it, and can agree upon a time, the governor may adjourn[1] or prorogue the court until that time. 2. If the two houses cannot agree as to the necessity or time of adjournment, the governor may adjourn or prorogue the court for such time as he thinks best, but not exceeding ninety days. 3. He may call a special session at any time when he thinks the public good requires it. 4. If from the prevalence of disease, or for any other cause, the governor thinks it unsafe for the court to meet in the usual place, he may change the place at his discretion.

2. Respecting Sessions of General Court.

The governor is the commander-in-chief of the military force of the State, having full power respecting its instruction and discipline. He may call out the troops, and lead them in case of invasion or insurrection, and may order out such portions as may be necessary to suppress riots, and to aid in enforcing the laws.

3. As Commander-in-Chief.

He has power, with advice of the council, to pardon offences against the Commonwealth, after persons have been convicted of the same; but this power does not extend to cases of impeachment. The pardoning power includes the right to remit a portion of the punishment, and to make such conditions and restrictions as are deemed best.

4. To Pardon.

[1] *Adjourn.*—As used in England, this word signifies to continue a session of parliament from day to day, while *prorogue* means to continue the parliament from one session to another. The words have essentially the same meaning in the constitution of Massachusetts.

The governor has power to appoint all judicial officers, medical-examiners, and notaries-public. There are also numerous boards and commissions established by the legislature, the members of which are appointed by the governor. In case of appointments, the consent of the council is required, and the governor must nominate a person at least seven days before the appointment. The commissions to military officers are issued by the governor.

5. To Appoint Officers.

The governor's warrant, drawn by consent of the council, is required for the payment of any money out of the treasury of the Commonwealth. These general powers are conferred by the constitution. There are numerous others connected with the details of administration, which are conferred by the General Court.

6. Warrant for Money.

The constitution provides that the governor shall have an honorable stated salary, of fixed and permanent value, established by standing laws, and amply sufficient to make him independent in his actions, to enable him to give the necessary time to the affairs of the State, and to maintain the dignity of the Commonwealth.

Salary.

THE LIEUTENANT-GOVERNOR.

There is annually elected a Lieutenant-Governor, whose title is His Honor. His qualifications are the same as those required of the governor; and he is elected and sworn at the same time and in the same way. He is a member of the council, and, in the absence of the governor, presides over its sessions. In case the chair of the governor is vacant by reason of death, or absence from the State, or otherwise, the lieutenant-governor performs the duties of the governor, and has all the powers which the constitution confers upon that officer.

THE EXECUTIVE COUNCIL.

Eight councillors are annually elected by the people of the State. After each census, the legislature divides the Commonwealth into eight districts, each comprising five contiguous senatorial districts; and one councillor is elected in each. He must have been an inhabitant of the Commonwealth five years next preceding his election. The members of the council take the required oaths at the same time as the governor. Vacancies in the council are filled by concurrent vote of the senate and house of representatives, or by the governor, if the legislature is not in session.

Election.

The duty of the council is to advise the governor in the administration of the government; and its advice is recorded and signed. Its consent is required to all executive appointments, and to warrants drawn for the payment of money. If, for any reason, there is a vacancy in the offices of governor and lieutenant-governor, a majority of the council have full power to do all that those officers might do. The council holds a regular meeting once a week. The governor, or, in his absence, the lieutenant-governor, presides.

Duties.

Sessions.

SECRETARY OF THE COMMONWEALTH.

The Secretary of the Commonwealth is chosen annually by the people. He must have been an inhabitant of the State five years next pre-

Election.

ceding his election. If the office becomes vacant during a session of the General Court, it is filled by joint ballot of the senators and representatives. If the vacancy occurs at any other time, it is filled by appointment by the governor. The secretary is sworn with the governor and council.

Duties.

The duties of the secretary are, to keep the records of the Commonwealth, to attest the signature of the governor on commissions and proclamations, and to affix thereto the state seal, of which he is the custodian. He also keeps the laws of the Commonwealth, and publishes them as has been stated. He submits to the General Court the reports of the various departments of the government, and publishes them as required by law. He furnishes to officers of the courts, and to certain county and town officers, blanks which they are required to fill out, and return to him, showing what has been done throughout the State by these subordinate officers in their several spheres. He also provides and issues the proper blanks, ballots, ballot-boxes and other apparatus used at elections. The results of elections are recorded at his office. Many statistics of public interest are also recorded by him. He has the power to appoint such deputies and clerks as the duties of the office make necessary.

TREASURER AND RECEIVER-GENERAL.

Election.

The provision of the constitution for the election, qualifications, and oath of the Treasurer is the same as for the secretary; and a vacancy in his office is filled in the same way as in the other.

This officer receives all money accruing to the State from taxation or otherwise; keeps all notes, bonds, and other securities which are the property of the Commonwealth; negotiates such loans as are authorized by the legislature; pays the interest on the debts of the State; and pays out such sums as the governor, with consent of the council, draws his warrant for. With the approbation of the governor and council, he invests the school fund. He has the custody of the weights, measures, and balances which are by law made the standard in the Commonwealth, and furnishes copies of them to the treasurer of each county, city, and town. He has power to employ such clerks as are necessary. No man is eligible to the office of Treasurer for more than five successive years. **Duties.**

AUDITOR.

The Auditor is chosen annually by the people under the same constitutional provision respecting election, qualifications, oaths, and vacancy, as the secretary and treasurer. Like them he may employ such assistance as is necessary, and like them also he is required to make to the legislature an annual report of his department with a detailed account of the expenses of the same. Thus the General Court controls the expenditure of the State. **Election.**

It is the duty of the auditor to examine all accounts and demands against the State, and to prepare a certificate of each, stating the amount due and the law authorizing its payment. On receiving this certificate, the governor draws his warrant for the money. Hence, to get money from the treasury of the Commonwealth, the following steps are necessary: **Duties.**

(1) an appropriation by act of the General Court; (2) an examination of the account by the auditor, and the issue of his certificate; (3) the signature of the governor, with consent of the council, to a warrant drawn on the treasury; (4) the presenting of the warrant to the treasurer.

Steps in Drawing Money.

Another duty of the auditor is, to keep an account of public receipts and expenditures, a statement of the school fund and other public property, and of all debts due to and from the Commonwealth. In his annual report, he gives a full statement of the financial condition of the Commonwealth, and an estimate of the income for the following year. It is also his duty annually to examine the accounts of the treasurer.

Other Duties.

ATTORNEY-GENERAL.

Besides the secretary, treasurer, and auditor, the people annually elect an Attorney-General, having the same qualifications as the others, and, like them, receiving for his services an annual salary determined by the legislature. His duty is, to appear for the Commonwealth in the supreme judicial court in all cases in which the Commonwealth is a party, and in such cases before any other court or tribunal when directed by the governor or either branch of the General Court. When public interest requires it, he also appears for the government in prosecutions for capital crime in the superior court.

He gives his opinion in writing upon all questions of law submitted to him by either branch of the legislature or by the governor and council. He advises the district attorneys in the discharge of their duties. He consults with the other executive officers, and advises them in matters pertaining to their official duties. He makes an annual report to the legislature of the cases conducted by him during the preceding year, with observations and suggestions upon the law of the State. He appoints several assistants.

BOARDS AND COMMISSIONERS.

In the administration of the public business, it is impossible for the governor immediately to superintend all the departments. Much of the work of supervision is committed to boards created by acts of the legislature, and consisting of persons appointed by the governor, and responsible to him.

Board of Education.

The Board of Education consists of the governor and lieutenant-governor, and eight persons appointed by the governor, each holding office eight years, and retiring each year in the order of appointment. The board has the supervision of the normal schools of the State. It also prescribes the form of registers to be kept in the public schools, and the form of blanks for school statistics; and annually reports to the legislature the condition of education within the State, with suggestions for improving it.

Secretary.

The board appoints a secretary, whose duties are, to collect information respecting the schools of the State, to diffuse throughout the State information as to the best means of improving the schools, to visit different parts of the State in order to awaken public interest in education, to preserve all documents relating to the educational interests of the State, to attend educational meetings. The board also appoints one or more *agents*, whose work is similar to that of the secretary. The secretary and agents annually hold teachers' institutes in different parts of the State, for the purpose of illustrating to teachers improved methods of instruction. The members of this board have no compensation for their services. The secretary and agents have salaries fixed by law.

Board of Agriculture.

The Board of Agriculture consists of the governor, lieutenant-governor, and secretary, three persons appointed by the governor, and one person appointed by each agricultural society of the State, and the president of the agricultural college. One-third of the appointed members retire annually, the term of service being three years. The duties of the board are, to learn how agriculture may be improved, and to make an annual report thereon. The board has power to fix the day on which the agricultural societies in the State may begin their exhibitions. The board appoints a secretary to visit the towns for the purpose of acquiring and giving information respecting the various departments of husbandry. This officer has a salary; but the members of the board receive no compensation.

Board of Health.

The Board of Health consists of seven persons, appointed by the governor for a term of seven years each. The general duties of this board concerning the public health are described in the following statute: "The board shall take cognizance of the interests of health and life among the citizens of this Commonwealth. They shall make sanitary investigations and inquiries in respect to the people, the causes of disease, and especially of epidemics and the sources of mortality, and the effects of localities, employment, conditions, and circumstances on the public health; and they shall gather such information in respect to those matters as they may deem proper for diffusion among the people. They shall advise the governor in regard to the location of any public institution." This board is entrusted with the enforcement of the laws against the adulteration of foods and drugs. It has also general supervision, with reference to their purity, of ponds and streams used as sources for public water supply.

Board of Insanity.

The State Board of Insanity consists of five persons appointed by the governor for the term of five years, one retiring annually. The board has general supervision of State hospitals and asylums for the insane, and all other institutions for insane or feeble-minded patients, either public or private. Two at least of the members must be experts in insanity. The board has power to investigate cases of commitment to asylums for alleged insanity, and may discharge persons whom it adjudges not to be insane, or who can be otherwise safely cared for. All questions as to the sanity of inmates of penal institutions of the Commonwealth are referred to this board for determination. The board appoints agents and subordinate officers.

Board of Charity.

The Board of Charity consists of nine persons appointed by the governor. It has general supervision of State almshouses and similar State institutions. The board also has charge of children found by the courts to be neglected by their parents, or growing up under circumstances exposing them to lead idle and dissolute lives. Good homes are found for such children if possible.

Prison Commissioners.

The Board of Prison Commissioners consists of three men and two women, appointed by the governor for a term of five years, one retiring annually. Their duties are, to superintend the classification and transfer of convicts, and to make rules and regulations for their discipline and employment, to inspect the jails and houses of correction of the State, and to make an annual report to the legislature. They have the general supervision of the State prison for men at Boston, the State reformatory for men at Concord, and the State reformatory for women at Sherborn, and make all needful rules and regulations for the management. They also, through an agent appointed for the purpose, seek to aid discharged convicts. This board has a secretary, who is a member and the executive officer, and who alone receives a salary.

Railroad Commissioners.

The Board of Railroad Commissioners consists of three members appointed by the governor for three years, one retiring annually. The duties are stated generally in the following statute: "Said commissioners shall have the general supervision of all railroads and railways, and shall examine the same, and keep themselves informed as to their condition, and the manner in which they are operated, with reference to the security and accommodation of the public." The commissioners are required to give notice to railroad corporations of any improvement which they think necessary to be made, to hear complaints of towns and cities against such corporations, and to investigate the cause of accidents. They may recommend and require the use by railroads and street railways of various appliances necessary to the safety of travellers and employees. The corporations are required to furnish to the commissioners any information concerning their business which they may demand.

The board also regulates to a certain extent the issue of stocks and bonds by the railroad companies. The members of this board receive salaries, which, together with all expenses, are assessed upon the corporations operating railroads within the State, in proportion to their income and profits for the year.

Harbor Commissioners.

The Board of Harbor and Land Commissioners consists of three persons appointed by the governor for a term of three years, one retiring annually. This board has "the general care and supervision of all the harbors and tide-waters, and of all the flats and lands flowed thereby within the Commonwealth, in order to prevent and remove unauthorized encroachments, and causes of every kind which are liable to interfere with the full navigation of said harbors, or in any way injure their channels, or cause any reduction of their tide-water." The board is authorized to direct in the building of bridges, wharves, and piers over tide-waters, and in the filling of flats; and no such work can be commenced until the plans are approved by the commissioners. The board also has general care and supervision of the Connecticut River within the limits of the Commonwealth. The members of the board receive a salary for their services, and their travelling expenses are also paid. An annual report is made to the legislature.

Gas and Electric Light Commissioners.

The Board of Gas and Electric Light Commissioners consists of three members appointed by the governor for the term of three years. This board has general supervision of all corporations engaged in the manufacture and sale of gas for lighting and fuel and in the sale of electric light. The board has the power to order any such company to reduce the price or improve the quality of the gas or electricity furnished to its consumers. The issue of stock by gas and electric companies is regulated by this commission, and such companies are required to make annual reports to the commission. The members receive an annual salary.

Insurance Commissioner.

An Insurance Commissioner is appointed by the governor for a term of three years. He is required to ascertain by personal examination the condition of all insurance companies doing business in the State; for which purpose he has free access to their books and papers. If any company appears to be insolvent, it is the duty of the commissioner to take proper legal measures to compel it to close its business. He furnishes blanks for the insurance returns, keeps a statement of the condition of each company, and makes an annual report to the legislature of the conduct and condition of the corporations examined, with suggestions concerning legislation. He receives an annual salary.

Board of Commissioners of Savings Banks.

The Board of Commissioners of Savings Banks consists of three members appointed by the governor for a term of three years. They are required to visit every savings bank in the State at least once in each year, and to examine thoroughly all its affairs. They have authority to inspect and examine trust companies and similar institutions. They keep a statement of the condition of each of these banks, and make an annual report thereof to the legislature. They are authorized to take measures to close the affairs of any such corporation which seems not to be able to meet its obligations. They receive an annual salary.

A Tax Commissioner, who also holds the office of commissioner of corporations, is appointed by the governor for the term of three years. As tax commissioner, his duties are largely connected with the taxing of corporations. He also furnishes information and advice to the assessors of cities and towns. As commissioner of corporations, he supervises the forming of corporations under the general laws of Massachusetts. He also receives and records reports as to the capital, officers, and other data concerning foreign corporations doing business within the Commonwealth.

Tax Commissioner.

The Board of Arbitration and Conciliation consists of three members appointed by the governor It is their duty to try to adjust disagreements and to aid in bringing about harmonious relations between employers and employed.

Board of Arbitration.

The Board of Bar Examiners examines and determines the fitness of all persons applying for the right to enter the practice of law.

Bar Examiners.

The Board of Registration in Medicine, the Board of Registration in Dentistry, and the Board of Registration in Pharmacy perform similar duties in the cases of persons applying for the right to follow the profession of medicine or dentistry or the occupation of a pharmacist respectively. All these boards are appointed by the governor, with the exception of the Board of Bar Examiners, the members of which are appointed by the Justices of the Supreme Courts.

Boards of Registration.

The commission consists of three persons appointed by the governor for the term of three years. It is their duty to construct highways in different parts of the State, and to collect use-

Highway Commission.

ful information regarding road-making for the use of counties, cities, and towns, with the general purpose of improving the highways of the Commonwealth. The members of this commission receive annual salaries.

Metropolitan Commissions.

The rapid increase of the population of Boston and the cities and towns immediately surrounding has resulted in a congested condition which has made it necessary to take concerted action to meet certain common needs in this thickly settled area, such as a system of sewerage, an adequate water supply, and parks. As this could not be done by the various municipalities without great lack of uniformity and constant conflict of authority, the legislature has provided for the establishment of a water and sewerage system for the joint use of a number of cities and towns within a radius of about ten miles of the city of Boston. This area is commonly called the Metropolitan District. These systems were constructed by boards appointed by the governor. The Metropolitan Water System and the Metropolitan Sewerage System are now under the control of a board called the Metropolitan Water and Sewerage Board, which consists of three members who are appointed by the governor and receive salaries. The Commonwealth has also provided for the construction and maintenance of parks and boulevards within this so-called metropolitan district, and these seashore and forest reservations are under the care and control of the Metropolitan Park Commission, which consists of five members appointed by the governor for the term of five years.

In addition to those that have been described, various commissions of a temporary nature are created from time to time. There are also various inspectors appointed by the governor to see that the laws of the State are obeyed. Among them are the inspectors of gas, fish, leather, and lumber. The several lunatic hospitals, and correctional and reformatory institutions, have each a board of trustees, or of inspectors, appointed by the governor.

District Police.

This body consists of a chief, and a number of officers, appointed by the governor for three years. There is a detective department and an inspection department. The members of the detective department have the general powers of police officers. They are required to aid the attorney-general, district attorneys, and magistrates in procuring evidence for the detection of crime and in the pursuit of criminals. The governor may call upon them to aid in preserving the peace. All local police officers are required to aid the State force in the discharge of their duties. It is the duty of the members of the inspection department to enforce the law as to the employment of women and minors in manufacturing, mechanical, and mercantile establishments, and the law as to ventilation and sanitation of factories and workshops. The members of the force receive annual salaries from the Commonwealth, and are forbidden to receive rewards or gifts on account of official services.

The Militia — Definition.

The word "militia" means a body of armed citizens trained to military duty, who may be called out in certain cases, but may not be kept in service like standing armies, in time of peace. The Constitution of the United States forbids any State to keep troops in time of peace ; but it allows the establishment of a militia. The militia of Massachusetts is of two kinds, described as *enrolled* and *active*.

Enrolled Militia. The enrolled militia consists of all able-bodied male citizens, resident within the State, of the age of eighteen years, and under the age of forty-five years, except idiots, lunatics, common drunkards, vagabonds, paupers, and convicted criminals, and a large number of persons holding office under the State and under the United States. Physicians, clergymen, judges and clerks of courts, sheriffs, firemen, railway conductors and engineers, and telegraph operators are also excepted. Quakers and Shakers, having conscientious scruples against bearing arms, are exempt. This enrolled militia is not subject to active duty, except in case of war, invasion, or riot. Then the governor may order out by draft or otherwise such numbers as he considers necessary, and organize them according to the laws of the Commonwealth.

Active Militia. The active militia is composed of volunteers. In case of war, invasion, riot, or to aid civil officers in executing the laws, this force is first ordered into service. At the time of the great fire in Boston in November, 1872, and in other similar cases, a part of the militia was ordered out to aid the civil officers in protecting property and preserving the peace. The various volunteer companies are scattered over the State, having armories for meeting and drill in the cities and larger towns. The companies are gathered into regiments and brigades. A portion of the volunteer militia is trained in the duties of seamanship for naval service. The militia is organized and disciplined according to United States regulations; but it is officered and trained under the laws of the Commonwealth.

The volunteer militia as such can be called upon for

State duty only, and is subject only to the orders of the State authorities, and cannot be ordered beyond the limits of the Commonwealth. When in 1861 and 1898 the President of the United States called for troops, the first to volunteer were members of the active militia. After being mustered into the service of the United States, the State regimental organizations were preserved in great extent, the officers continuing to serve in the same rank as before.

Officers. The governor exercises his power as commander-in-chief through his staff, which consists of a number of military officers, all appointed by himself. The election or appointment of other officers is regulated by law; but all commissions are issued by the governor.

Equipments. The State provides such uniforms, arms, and equipments as are necessary; but they remain the property of the State, and can be taken away at any time. The expense of armories for the various companies is also borne by the State. The militia is obliged by law to spend a prescribed amount of time in drill and camp-duty; for which time compensation is given by the Commonwealth according to law. To preserve the peace, the militia may be ordered out by the governor, or, in certain cases, by the mayor of a city, a justice, or a sheriff.

It will be seen that the military force of the Commonwealth is under the direction and control of the governor, and is therefore a branch of the executive department. But, since all appropriations for its support must be made by the General Court, it can never become an instrument of tyranny. Thus the legislative department holds a check upon the governor.

SUMMARY.

The executive department is thus constituted: —

His Excellency the Governor,
His Honor the Lieutenant-Governor,
The Council,
The Secretary of the Commonwealth,
The Treasurer and Receiver-General,
The Auditor,
The Attorney-General,
The Governor's Staff,
The Board of Education,
The Board of Agriculture,
The Board of Health,
The Board of Insanity,
The Board of Charity,
The Board of Prison Commissioners,
The Board of Railroad Commissioners,
The Board of Harbor and Land Commissioners,
The Board of Gas and Electric Light Commissioners,
The Insurance Commissioner,
The Board of Commissioners of Savings Banks,
The Tax Commissioner,
The Board of Arbitration and Conciliation,
The Board of Bar Examiners,
The Boards of Registration in Medicine, Dentistry, and Pharmacy,
The Highway Commission,
The Metropolitan Commissions,
The District Police,
The Militia.

CHAPTER XX.

THE JUDICIAL DEPARTMENT.

Power to Establish.

The Constitution gives to the legislature the power to constitute such courts of justice as may be necessary. The judicial department consists of a number of such courts established by statute, and having their powers carefully defined.

Judges.

The judges are appointed by the governor, with the consent of the council. They hold office during good behavior, but may be removed by the governor, with consent of the council, upon the address of both branches of the legislature or by impeachment.

Supreme Judicial Court.

The Supreme Judicial Court consists of one chief and six associate justices. Four justices constitute a quorum. Sessions for the decision of questions of law, called *law sittings*, are held in Boston, and in some of the counties; five justices sit at these sessions; and sessions for the trial of causes by jury, called *jury sittings*, are held by a single justice at prescribed times in each county.

Superior Court.

The Superior Court consists of a chief and seventeen associate justices. The sittings, and places for holding its sittings, are prescribed by law; but at least two sittings are held annually in each county. This court has original jurisdiction[1] of all crimes and misdemeanors, and appellate[2] jurisdiction of all offences tried and determined before a police court, a district court, or trial justices. In criminal causes, its decision is final, unless exceptions are taken to some decisions of law. It has also appellate jurisdiction over a large number of civil causes, and original jurisdiction over some. Certain causes may be removed from this court to the Supreme Court on appeal, on questions of law, and on motion, when the amount in controversy is large. Trials for capital crimes are held in the Superior Court before a jury and two justices. This court also has jurisdiction in cases of divorce.

Probate Court.

In each county of the Commonwealth, a Probate Court is established by law. It consists of a judge,[3] appointed as are other judicial officers. The times and places of holding the court session are fixed by law. These courts have jurisdiction of the probate[4] of wills, and administration of estates,[5] of the appointment of guardians to minors and others; of all matters relating to the settlement of

[1] *Original jurisdiction*, authority to take the first steps in a legal procedure.

[2] *Appellate jurisdiction*, authority to reconsider, by a new trial, causes that have been determined by another court. A demand for such new trial is called an appeal.

[3] The counties of Suffolk and Middlesex have each two judges.

[4] The *probate* of a will is the proof before the proper officer that an instrument purporting to be the last will and testament of a deceased person is really such. The carrying out the provisions of the will is intrusted to a person, or persons, named in the instrument as executors.

[5] *Administration*, the settlement of the estate of a deceased person who has left no will. The deceased in such a case is said to have died *intestate;* and an administrator is appointed by the judge of probate, usually on petition. If no executor is named in a will, an administrator is appointed.

estates of deceased persons and wards; of petitions for adoption of children, and change of name; and of petitions for partition of real estate among tenants in common. Appeals may be had to the Supreme Judicial Court on questions of law and some questions of fact, that being the supreme court of probate. In certain cases appeals on questions of fact may be had to the Superior Court.

Police Courts.

Police Courts are established in certain cities and large towns; each consisting of a justice, who receives an annual salary, and two special justices, who hold courts in the absence of the justice, and receive compensation for actual service. Daily sessions are held for criminal causes. These courts have jurisdiction in civil causes where the amount at issue does not exceed one thousand dollars, and in criminal causes where the law allows but a small fine or a short imprisonment. In all these cases, appeals are allowed to the Superior Court.

District Courts.

District Courts are established in different parts of the Commonwealth, having the same number of justices, and the same jurisdiction, as the police courts. Each district consists of a group of towns; and the times and places for holding the sessions are prescribed by law.

Municipal Court of Boston.

This court has jurisdiction to the amount of two thousand dollars, has a chief justice, seven associates, and two special justices; has jurisdiction over the central portion of the city, and is called the Municipal Court of the City of Boston. There are a number of Municipal District Courts in the outlying districts of Boston, each having jurisdiction over its particular section. Each of these courts has one justice and two special justices, and about the same jurisdiction as police courts.

Court of Registration. The Court of Registration consists of a judge and an assistant judge, each appointed by the governor. This court also has a clerical officer called a recorder. The Court of Registration has power upon application of a person owning land in Massachusetts to cause an examination to be made of his title to the land, and if after examination and upon proper proceedings the court is satisfied that the applicant possesses a good and valid title to the land in question, it registers and confirms his title thereto.

Justices of the Peace. Justices of the peace once formed a large and important class of judicial officers. They are appointed by the governor, with consent of the council, for a term of seven years, and may be reappointed. They have authority to administer oaths in all cases required by law, and a few justices are specially authorized by the governor to join persons in marriage. When specially commissioned to do so, they may issue warrants and summonses and may take bail. These are only fragments of the powers once possessed. In earlier days in England and Massachusetts they had authority to cause the arrest of disturbers of the peace, to try them and pass sentence on them, or in the case of aggravated offences to hold them for trial by a higher court. They also had authority to try small civil causes. Since the population has become more dense, the municipal and district courts have taken the more important functions.

Trial Justices. A certain number of justices of the peace in each county are commissioned as trial justices for a term of three years. In addition to their functions as justices of the peace, they have criminal jurisdiction of such offences as breaches of the peace, petty larcenies and trespass, gambling, and in general those to which the statutes affix a fine not exceeding fifty dollars, or an imprisonment not exceeding six months. They have civil jurisdiction in cases where the amount is very small.

Clerk of Courts.

Each of the courts that have been described, except trial justices, and some of the district courts, has a clerk whose duties are, to attend its sessions, to preserve its papers, to keep a record of its proceedings, and to issue writs in its name. The clerk of the Supreme Judicial Court for the Commonwealth is appointed by that court for a term of five years. An assistant clerk is also appointed in the same way for three years. In each county a clerk of courts is elected once in five years. He acts as clerk of the Supreme Judicial Court for its terms in the counties,[1] as clerk of the Superior Court, and as clerk of the county commissioners. The clerks of the district, police, and municipal courts are appointed by the governor for a term of five years.

Attorneys.

Attorneys-at-law are officers of the courts. They are employed to manage civil and criminal causes for the parties concerned in them. In Massachusetts, an attorney must be either a citizen of the State, or an alien who has declared his intention of becoming a citizen. He must be an inhabitant of the State, at least twenty-one years of age, and of good moral character. He must have a sufficiently extensive knowledge of law to pass an acceptable examination before the Board of Bar Examiners.

[1] Except in Suffolk.

Admission to Practice. A person desiring to be admitted to practice must apply to the Superior or Supreme Judicial Court, and must in open court take and subscribe oaths to support the Constitution of the United States and of the Commonwealth, and the following oath of office: "You solemnly swear that you will do no falsehood, nor consent to the doing of any in court; you will not wittingly or willingly promote or sue any false, groundless, or unlawful suit, nor give aid or consent to the same; you will delay no man for lucre or malice; but you will conduct yourself in the office of an attorney within the courts, according to the best of your knowledge and discretion, and with all good fidelity, as well to the courts as your clients. So help you God." Attorneys may be removed by the court for deceit, malpractice, or other gross misconduct.

Reporter. Connected with the Supreme Judicial Court is an officer called a Reporter, who is appointed by the governor and council, and removable at their pleasure. He is required to attend the court personally at all the law terms and capital trials, and to make true reports of decisions on all legal questions argued by counsel. These reports contain what has before been spoken of as court-law, in distinction from statute-law.

District Attorneys. The Commonwealth is divided into eight districts for the administration of criminal justice; and in each of these a District Attorney is elected by the people once in three years. These officers appear for the Commonwealth to prosecute cases in the superior criminal courts. They aid the attorney-general in capital cases, and in arguing exceptions in other criminal cases.

JURIES.

A jury is a body of men sworn to declare the facts of a case from the evidence and the law presented to them. The qualifications of jurors, their duties and privileges, and the manner in which they are called to service, are regulated by statutes.

Qualifications. In Massachusetts, all persons qualified to vote for representatives to the General Court are liable to be called as jurors, excepting certain classes legally exempted. These are State, county, and national officers, professional men, bank-cashiers, militia-men, and firemen and persons more than sixty-five years of age. Persons are not liable to service as jurors oftener than once in three years; except in Nantucket and Dukes Counties, where they may be called to service once in two years.

Jury List and Box. The selectmen of each town and the registrars of voters in cities annually prepare a list of such persons not exempt, as they think qualified to serve as jurors, being persons of good moral character and sound judgment. This list includes not less than one for every hundred, and not more than one for every sixty inhabitants. The list is posted in public places for at least ten days, after which it is presented to the town at a meeting, for revision and acceptance. Names may be added or taken off by vote of the town. After acceptance by the town, the names on the list are written each on a separate paper. These are then folded with the name inside, and placed in a box kept for the purpose.

Previous to the beginning of each sitting of the Supreme and Superior Courts, the clerk issues a writ to the sheriff, calling from each town and city a number of jurors in proportion to its inhabitants. This writ is served on the town clerk and selectmen.

Summoning and Drawing Jurors.

These officials then meet; and one of the selectmen proceeds to draw from the box as many papers as are required. If any person whose name is drawn is exempt by law, or unable to attend on account of sickness or absence, or has served as juror within three years, his name is replaced, and another drawn. When the name is drawn, and the person serves, the date of drawing is indorsed upon the paper; and it is then returned to the box. The constable notifies persons whose names are drawn, and informs them of the time when the court begins its session. Thirty jurors are summoned to each session. A person neglecting to attend, when legally drawn and summoned, is liable to a fine.

In cities the mayor and aldermen exercise the powers of the town in the revision of jury lists and the drawing of juries.

Highway Jury.

A Highway Jury consists of twelve men, drawn in the usual way for the purpose of deciding questions of damage in connection with the laying-out or alteration of roads. Such a jury is called at the request of parties aggrieved by a decision of the county commissioners. Upon a petition for a jury, these officers issue a warrant to the sheriff to summon the requisite number from the three nearest towns. In certain cases, where parties are dissatisfied with orders of selectmen regarding buildings considered as nuisances, and regarding steam-engines, and in cases connected with the flowage of lands, juries such as have last been described may be called to decide the matter. This is commonly called a Sheriff's Jury.

OUTLINE OF JUDICIAL PROCEDURE.

Parties.

An illustrative example will serve to show the relation of the various branches of the judiciary department to each other and to the public. Every action or suit at law supposes two parties: one, called the *plaintiff*, who brings the charge upon which the action is based; the other, called the *defendant*, against whom the charge is brought.

Classes of Actions.

Suits at law are either civil or criminal. A civil action has for its object the restoration of property, the recovery of private rights, or compensation for their infraction. Such are suits brought to recover a debt, or to obtain money for an injury sustained upon a highway. A criminal action has for its object the punishment of an individual for a violation of law. In such actions the government is always the plaintiff; the person complaining of the wrongful act is called the complainant. Civil actions, if successful, result in the payment of money or the restoration of property or rights by the defendant to the plaintiff. Criminal actions, if successful, result in the infliction of a penalty upon the defendant: either a fine paid to the government, or imprisonment, or both.

Criminal Actions.

We will proceed to notice the ordinary steps in the conduct of a criminal action. Suppose that in some town in the Commonwealth a man enters a store in the daytime and steals therefrom a watch. In course of the judicial proceedings that might arise, the *complaint* would be first in order.

Complaint.

This would be a written instrument, stating formally, but specifically, the name and residence of the person accused, the nature of the crime itself, with the time and place of its commission, and requesting that he be apprehended for trial. This must be sworn to by the complainant before some trial justice or court; and he must offer some evidence for his suspicion against the person accused. This complaint is the foundation of the whole course of proceeding.

Warrant.

The justice next issues a *warrant*. This is a command to the sheriff of the county, or his deputy, or any constable of the town, to apprehend the person named in the complaint, and bring him before some trial justice or court to answer to the complaint. The warrant specifies the offence, and also directs the officer to summon certain persons as witnesses against the defendant. If the offence is a trivial one, the defendant may be summoned to appear in court without arrest.

Return.

The officer, having made the arrest, appears before the justice with his prisoner, and makes a *return* of his warrant. This is a short statement of the manner in which the command has been executed. It is written on the back of the instrument, and signed by the officer. A detailed account of charges is also rendered.

Recognizance.

The justice then appoints a time for the examination, and the accused may be admitted to *bail;* that is, he may be delivered to persons who give security that he shall appear at the specified time, to answer to the complaint. These persons are said to recognize, or give a *recognizance*, which is a written obligation to pay a certain sum of money if a specified condition is not complied with. If the accused can find no person willing to become surety for his appearance, he is kept in custody, or the sureties may surrender him to the authorities at any time.

Meanwhile, at his request, the justice issues what is called a *subpœna* to each of such persons as the defendant wishes to testify in his behalf. This instrument requires the individual named to appear at a certain time and place, to give evidence in the case. The names of the complainant and of the defendant are specified.

Subpœna.

At the appointed time, the accused is brought before the justice. If the value of the property stolen is less than a certain amount specified by statute, the justice has *final jurisdiction;* that is, he may, if the crime is proved, pass sentence, and make the necessary orders for carrying it into effect. If the value is greater than the legal limit, the justice examines the accused, and, if the evidence is sufficient, requires him to give a recognizance to appear before the Superior Court to await the action of the Grand Jury. In this case, the justice has only *initial jurisdiction.*

Jurisdiction.

The parties being in the presence of the justice, the *arraignment* takes place. The defendant rises; the justice or clerk reads to him the complaint, and asks him what he says to it,—"Guilty," or "Not guilty." His answer is the *plea.* If he pleads "Guilty," sentence may be passed at once. If he pleads "Not guilty," evidence is then presented tending to prove his guilt.

Arraignment.

Plea.

The witnesses for the government are called, and standing, and raising their right hands, swear to tell the truth, the whole truth, and nothing but the truth. They are then called sepa-

Testimony.

rately; and each tells what he knows of the case. After this examination of the witness, he is cross-examined, as it is called, by the counsel for the defendant; whose aim is, to destroy the effect of his testimony by involving him in contradictions, or by showing his incapacity. After all the evidence is presented against the party, the witnesses for the defence are called and sworn, and examined separately, first by the defendant's counsel, then by the representative of the government.

Arguments of Counsel. When all the evidence upon both sides has been heard, the counsel for the defendant proceeds to make an argument in his favor based upon the evidence adduced. This argument is frequently, but improperly, called a plea.

Sentence. The justice, having heard the evidence and the argument, considers the case, and passes judgment upon it. He declares the defendant guilty, and pronounces the sentence; or not guilty, and releases him.

Costs. The penalty may be a fine and *costs*. The statutes determine the limit of the fine, and regulate the charges which are included under the title "costs." These are, the fees of the justice unless he has a salary, of the officer for serving the warrant and summons, and of the witnesses.

Commitment. In case the fine and costs are not paid, the convicted man may be committed to jail until they are paid, or for a specified number of days if he is unable to pay.

Appeal. This would end the proceedings in a district or police court; but, if the defendant is not satisfied with the decision, he may appeal to the Superior Court. In this case, he is required to bring sureties, who give their recognizance for him to appear before the higher court to prosecute his appeal. This would secure him a new trial before a jury. The features of a jury trial will now be presented.

Examination.

In the case that has been considered, if the crime had been beyond the jurisdiction of the justice, an examination of the witnesses would have taken place. If the justice thought that the evidence afforded probable cause to believe him guilty, he would require him to furnish bail for his appearance at the next term of the higher court; or, if he could not find bail, would commit him to jail meanwhile. The justice or clerk would then send the complaint, with a record of the proceedings thereon, to the Superior Court.

Grand Jury.

Previous to the beginning of a criminal term of the Superior Court, twenty-three of the persons who have been drawn as jurors, being those first drawn, present themselves before the judge who is to hold the court, and take an oath, diligently, and without fear or favor, to inquire into such cases as may be brought before them, and to keep their deliberations secret. This body is the Grand Jury. The court gives it directions as to its duties. The members choose a foreman and a clerk.

Indictment.

The district attorney prepares a formal accusation against the person whom we have supposed under recognizance to appear at the Superior Court. This instrument is called an *indictment*, and specifies the name and residence of the party, and the crime with which he is charged. Witnesses in support of the charge are sworn and heard, but none for the defence. If twelve of the jury agree that the person should be brought to trial, the foreman indorses upon the indictment the words, "A true bill," and signs it. If the jury think there is not sufficient ground for the accusation, the foreman writes, "Not found," and signs it. This instrument forms the basis of action in the Superior Court, as the complaint does in the lower court.

Challenge.

When the time arrives for the trial, a list of twelve jurors is read by the clerk, the names being drawn from a box. Exception may be taken to any of these by the accused or by the government, on the ground of character, incompetency, or prejudice. This objection is called a *challenge*. The accused may challenge *two* jurors *peremptorily;* that is, without assigning cause. Other names are substituted, until the number twelve is complete. Each member then swears that he will well and truly try the issue between the Commonwealth and the defendant, according to the law and the evidence. This body is called a *petit* jury. Its business is to hear the evidence, and then decide whether the accused is guilty, or not, of the crime specified in the indictment.

Charge.

The steps in the trial are similar to those in the lower court,[1]—the arraignment, the plea, the testimony, the arguments. After the case has been presented to the jury by both sides, the judge makes his *charge* to the jury, in which he explains the law bearing upon the case, and indicates to them the principles that should guide them in making their decision.

[1] In the Superior Court all criminal cases are prosecuted by the district-attorney, and are tried by jury.

The jury then retire, in charge of the sheriff, for consultation. They are kept by themselves until they make up their opinion. If they are unanimous in that opinion, they return to the court-room, where the foreman announces the verdict; which must be "Guilty," or "Not guilty." If the jury cannot agree after long deliberation, they may be discharged; in which case, a new trial would be necessary. If the verdict is "Guilty," the court pronounces the sentence which the law requires. If the verdict is "Not guilty," the person can never be tried again for the same offence.

Verdict.

If the penalty is imprisonment, the person is committed to the sheriff to be lodged in the designated place of confinement; if a fine, legal steps are taken to secure its payment.

Sentence.

The case may not end here. During the trial, objections may have been made to the admission of certain evidence. The judge has ruled that it may be admitted. The counsel takes exceptions to the ruling of the judge. If the judge allows the exceptions, they are properly framed, and go to the full bench of the Supreme Judicial Court at a law term; where arguments are made by the counsel on both sides. If the court sustains the ruling of the judge, the case is remanded to the Superior Court for sentence. If the ruling is not sustained, a new trial is had at some future term of the Superior Court.

Exceptions.

There is more diversity in procedure in civil than in criminal actions. A simple case may serve to illustrate the chief points of difference between them. Suppose a man has sold merchandise to the value of a hundred dollars, for which he has

Civil Actions.

received no pay. He purposes to sue for the recovery of the debt. The first step is to obtain a *writ*. This is an order to a sheriff or other officer, directing him to attach the property of the debtor to a specified amount, and to summon the debtor to appear before the justice at a certain time and place, to answer to the demand of the plaintiff. The officer, in obedience to this writ, takes possession of the property, and holds it in custody until judgment upon the case has been rendered by the court. The writ may also direct the arrest of the party, if the plaintiff has made affidavit according to law before a designated officer, and received from him a certificate authorizing the arrest of the defendant. In certain cases, a man may escape or be released from arrest by taking what is called "the poor debtor's oath," or an oath that he does not intend to leave the State. These oaths, and the manner of taking them, are prescribed by statute. Each writ specifies the day on which it shall be returned; and this return is made, as in the case of the warrant, by an indorsement by the officer, stating what he has done.

The Writ. **Attachment.** **Summons.**

The next step in the process is the *pleading*. This is a formal and legal statement of the facts which constitute the plaintiff's cause of action, followed by a similar statement of the facts which constitute the defendant's ground of defence. Thus the plaintiff may declare the time and mode of the sale, and the quality and amount and value of the goods. The defendant may deny the purchase, or assert that payment has been made in whole or in part, or on some other ground plead against the obligation.

Pleading.

When some fact is asserted by one party, and denied by the other, an *issue* is thereby made, and the trial begins. Witnesses are called, sworn, and testify first for the plaintiff, then for the defendant. The arguments follow, and then the judgment. If the justice decides for the plaintiff, and the debt is not paid, a writ of *execution* is issued.

Trial.

This directs the officer to take of the property of the defendant, and obtain such sums as are necessary to satisfy the judgment and the expenses. This is usually done by sale by auction. If the sale produces more than the amount required, the balance is paid to the owner. As in criminal actions, appeal may be taken to a higher court, where the steps would be similar, except that the jury would decide upon the question at issue if a jury trial was claimed by either party. It will be seen that the terms "attachment" and "execution" belong exclusively to civil actions.

Execution.

IMPEACHMENT.

In the Constitution of Massachusetts, as in all the States, provision is made for removal from public offices by a process called impeachment. This may be defined as a written accusation against a civil officer, made in a constitutional way, for maladministration of office.

Definition.

Neither the Constitution nor the statutes of Massachusetts specify what officers may be impeached; but, according to precedent established by the Congress of the United States, it may be supposed that those executive officers of the Commonwealth who are elected by the people, and all judicial officers, are liable to the process.

Who may be Impeached.

Process. Impeachments can only be brought by the house of representatives; and they are tried by the senate. If an officer is supposed guilty of wrong-doing in connection with his office, the representatives may appoint a committee to investigate. This committee may report in favor of impeachment. If the representatives so decide, a committee is appointed to prepare articles of impeachment, and present them to the senate.

Trial. The articles having been presented, the person is summoned to appear, and answer to the charges. Each senator takes an oath "well and truly to try the charges;" and the trial is conducted according to the usual procedure in other courts. A majority of the senators present is required for conviction.

Judgment. Judgment, in case of conviction, may extend to removal from office, and disqualification to hold any office of trust, honor, or profit under the Commonwealth. The person is also liable to trial and punishment for the crime before the proper courts, in accordance with the laws of the State.

SUMMARY.

The Judicial Department is constituted as follows: —

Senate, as a court to try impeachment,
Supreme Judicial Court,
Superior Court,
Probate Court,
Court of Registration,
Police and District Courts,
Trial Justices,
Clerk of Courts,
Reporter of Supreme Judicial Court,
Attorneys,
Juries.

CHAPTER XXI.

COUNTIES.

History of.

As early as the time of the Saxons, England was divided into districts for convenience in the administration of justice. The most important of these was the *shire*, as it was called, from a Saxon word meaning *to cut*. The shire was a part cut off. In Norman times, the shire took the name *county*, from the word *count*, a Norman title of nobility.

For a few years after the settlement of Massachusetts, as we have seen, justice was administered by the General Court and the Court of Assistants, and by local magistrates in the towns; but, as soon as the colony increased its territory and population, the people adopted the English institution of the county, by grouping the towns together, and setting up county courts.

In 1643 four counties were formed: Suffolk, comprising Boston and the towns south of it; Essex, the towns east of Boston; Middlesex, those north of Boston; and Norfolk, consisting of the towns of New Hampshire, which had been united to Massachusetts. After the separation of the two colonies, those towns that came within the Massachusetts line were united to Essex; and the name Norfolk was given to the towns comprising the present Norfolk County.

Previous to the union of Plymouth with Massachusetts, that colony had established the counties of Plymouth, Barnstable, and Bristol. The other counties were established as follows: Worcester, in 1731, from parts of other counties; Hampshire, in 1662, comprising those towns on the Connecticut early settled from Massachusetts Bay; Berkshire, from Hampshire, in 1761; Hampden and Franklin, from Hampshire, in 1811; Dukes, given to the Duke of York in 1664, and joined to New York, made a county in 1685, and united to Massachusetts by the Province charter; Nantucket, formed in 1695.

Definition.

As now constituted in Massachusetts, a county may be defined as a corporate body,[1] consisting of a group of adjacent towns, organized, under the direction of the State, for convenience in the administration of justice.

Property.

Each county is obliged to own and maintain suitable court-houses, jails, and buildings for the registry and preservation of deeds, wills, and court records. The town in which these buildings are situated, and where the courts are held, is called the shire town. Some counties have more than one.

Officers.

Counties, as such, have no legislative power: hence their officers are chiefly executive. The number and duty of these officers are prescribed by law, and are the same throughout the State.

[1] A *corporate* body, or *corporation*, is a body consisting of one or more individuals, established by law, usually for some specific purpose, and continued by a succession of members. This body has a name, and under that name may sue and be sued, may hold and dispose of property, may have a common seal, may choose officers, and make by-laws for its government and administration. The body may be created by a special law called a charter; or it may organize under some general statute.

In each county, three commissioners are chosen by the people for three years, one retiring annually; and two special commissioners are chosen every three years.[1] These commissioners are empowered to provide for erecting and repairing the county buildings; to have the care of the county property; to represent the county in suits at law; to apportion the county taxes among the towns; to lay out, alter, and discontinue highways within the county, upon petition of parties interested, and after a suitable hearing; to have charge of Houses of Correction in the county, appointing the keepers, making rules, and providing supplies. If either of the commissioners is personally interested in any matter before them, one of the special commissioners takes his place for the time. Thus a commissioner cannot act upon a highway question within his own town. The salaries of these officers, and the time and place of meeting in each county, are fixed by statute.

County Commissioners.

In each county, a Treasurer[2] is elected by the people for a term of three years. He is sworn, and gives bonds for the faithful discharge of his duties, and receives an annual salary fixed by law. The treasurer receives and pays out, under the direction of the commissioners, all money belonging to the county. This includes that raised by taxation, and whatever comes from the payment of fines and costs in the various courts. This officer also has the charge of

Treasurer.

[1] The aldermen of Boston, and the selectmen of Nantucket, have the powers and duties of commissioners in their respective counties. In Suffolk, the county buildings are provided by the city of Boston.

[2] The treasurers of the city of Boston and of the town of Nantucket act as treasurers of their respective counties.

a set of the standard weights and measures furnished by the Commonwealth for the use of the county.

Register of Deeds. Each county has one or more Registers of Deeds. If one, he is elected by the people of the county. If more than one, the county is divided by law into districts, in each of which a register is elected by the people. The term of office is three years. The officers are under oath and bonds. Their offices are in the shire-towns; and their duty is, to receive and record, according to methods prescribed by law, all deeds and mortgages brought to them for the purpose. In the early history of the county, all transfers of land were made publicly at the county courts to prevent fraud. The registry is designed to serve the same purpose by making all such transfers a matter of record, so that the legal title to any land in the county may be readily ascertained.

Register of Probate. In each county, a Register of Probate is elected by the people every five years. He has the care of all books and papers pertaining to the business of the probate court. He may receive and keep any wills that may be deposited in the office, giving a certificate therefor. He is under oath and bonds, and is forbidden by law to be interested as counsel, executor, administrator, or otherwise officially, in any matter pending in the courts. In some of the counties, an assistant register is appointed by the probate judge for a term of three years.

Sheriff. The oldest county-officer is the Sheriff. In the earliest history of the county, this officer, called the *shire-reeve*, shared the administration of county business with the alderman and bishop. Later, the civil functions devolved entirely upon him. presided at the county court, and was responsible for the public peace. Formerly, in England, he was elected by the people; now he is appointed by the king for one year, and during that time is the highest personage in the county, taking precedence of noblemen.

History.

In Massachusetts, the people of each county elect a sheriff once in three years. He is popularly termed the high sheriff, and appoints deputies, for whom he is responsible. Both the sheriff and his deputies are under oath and bonds for the faithful discharge of their duties.

Deputies.

The Sheriff's first duty is to preserve the peace within his county. To this end he may apprehend and commit to prison all persons who break the peace. He is bound to pursue and take all such criminals as murderers, robbers, and rioters. He has the safe keeping of the county jail, and is responsible for the custody of the prisoners confined therein, the jailer being his deputy. In the exercise of these duties, the sheriff may demand the assistance of the inhabitants of the county. Any person who refuses aid when thus called upon is liable to fine and imprisonment. As the population becomes concentrated in cities and large towns the sheriff has less to do in the preservation of the peace, that duty being performed by the local police.

Duties.

1. Preserving Peace.

The Sheriff is required to attend all county courts, and the meetings of the county commissioners when so ordered by the Board. During the term of the court, he has charge of the prisoners on trial, of the witnesses, and of the juries. It is his business to see that the sentence of the court is carried into execution, either by collecting the fines,

2. Attending Courts.

or placing the convicted person in the designated place of confinement. The death sentence for capital crimes is executed by the warden of the state prison.

3. Serving Processes.

The Sheriff is required to serve, either by himself or his deputies, all writs and processes that may be lawfully issued to him within his county by any of the courts of justice. In obedience to an order from the clerk of the court, he summons the juries from their respective towns and cities through the local constables.

Medical Examiners.

In each county two or more persons are appointed by the governor to examine the bodies of persons who are supposed to have come to their death by violence. They are called Medical Examiners and hold office for seven years. If the examiner thinks the death was caused by violence he files a copy of the record of his examination with the district attorney, and another with the district, police, or municipal court, or a trial justice. The justice or court then holds an inquest to determine by what means the person came to his death. This takes the place of the coroner's inquest which was formerly held in such cases. An inquest is held in all cases of death by accident upon any railroad.

SUMMARY OF COUNTY OFFICERS.

Three Commissioners, elected for three years.

Two Special Commissioners,	elected	for	three	years.
Treasurer,	"	"	"	"
Register of Deeds,	"	"	"	"
Register of Probate,	"	"	five	"
Sheriff,	"	"	three	"
Medical Examiners, appointed by governor,			seven	"

CHAPTER XXII.

TOWNS.

In the Saxon period of English history, the freemen were grouped into little bodies of ten householders each, called *tithings;* and these were again united into organizations called *hundreds.* The next larger group was the county. These smaller divisions were for the more perfect administration of justice, each body being responsible for its members. If a person had committed a crime, his tithing was bound to produce him to the court; or, failing to do so, was required to pay a specified sum of money. The effect of this system was to throw the burden of local administration directly upon the people of the district. Each body had interests peculiar to itself; and, to promote these, there must be free discussion and choice of individuals to represent them. After the introduction of the feudal system, these smaller institutions fell into disuse; but, in the towns, the idea of local self-government was retained, and was brought to this country by the early settlers of New England.

Origin.

The people, settling together in different localities, formed distinct communities, called plantations, and, from the beginning, were in

Plantations.

the habit of meeting to consider matters of common interest. Very early, the magistrates came to recognize these communities as such, defined carefully the boundaries of land which each should occupy, and, to each community occupying such portion of territory, gave a name. The court, from time to time, gave permission to form new settlements, fixing the boundaries, and giving a name.

Growth of Powers. The charter gave all power of government to the General Court; but that body early gave its sanction to a practice which had grown up in the towns, of managing their own local affairs through men chosen for this purpose, called *selectmen*. From time to time, the towns were empowered to choose other municipal officers, and gradually came to have those powers and duties which are now defined by the general statutes; but the supreme jurisdiction remained with the General Court, which has always considered the towns as corporations, and prescribed the mode in which they should perform their functions. It is through the town governments that the State brings its authority directly to bear upon the people. Its taxes are received by the town collector, its writs of election and of judicial process served by town constables, and its school-laws executed by town committee-men.

Influence. This township system was essentially the same in all the New England colonies. Its influence has been great. The grouping of the people in towns afforded opportunity for frequent intercourse and exchange of opinion. It made it possible to support regular services of public worship, and to establish and maintain public schools. The frequent meetings of the freemen of the towns gave to all an opportunity to become acquainted with the conduct of public affairs, and cultivated a spirit of independence in thought and action. In them every man, without distinction, was free to make the best use of all his talents; and so they were the schools in which the men were trained who were foremost in discussing the great questions that preceded the Revolution. At the same time, the whole body of the people were prepared to judge and act upon these subjects when the occasion came. Similar influences have been exerted by these organizations to the present time.

Definition.

A town is a body corporate, occupying a definite portion of territory, and exercising local jurisdiction under the control of the State.

Powers.

As has been said, the powers of a town are defined by general statutes. They are as follows: to sue and be sued; to hold and dispose of real and personal property for the public use of the inhabitants; to make such contracts and orders as are necessary for the exercise of their corporate powers; to make such by-laws as are necessary for managing their affairs, and for preserving peace and good order; to raise money by taxation.

Purposes for which Money may be Raised.

Money may be raised by taxation for the support of town schools, for the care of the poor, for highways, for burial grounds, for maintaining a fire department, for destroying noxious animals, for preparing town histories, for public libraries, for planting shade-trees, for the preservation of the peace and the detection of offenders, for soldiers' monuments, for repairing and decorating soldiers' graves, for aiding disabled soldiers and sailors and the families of the slain, for all other necessary charges.

Town Meetings. Every town is required by law to hold an annual meeting in February, March, or April. At this time, the officers are chosen, and the annual appropriations made. Other meetings may be held at such times as the selectmen may order.

Warrant. Every town meeting is held under a warrant signed by the selectmen, directed to a constable, requiring him to notify the legal voters of the town to meet at a specified place and time, to act upon matters specified in the warrant. The constable, having received the warrant, serves it as the by-laws of the town direct, usually by posting attested copies of it in several public places, at least seven days before the date of the meeting. The constable returns the warrant to the town-clerk, indorsing upon it the fact that he has served it properly. This warrant, with the officer's return, is read at the opening of the meeting, and forms the legal basis of all the town's action. No action is legal upon subjects not specified in the warrant. The whole action of a meeting is invalid if the warrant has not been served legally. The legislature is sometimes called upon to legalize the action of a town meeting. Each meeting is called to order by the town-clerk, who reads the warrant, and presides during the choice of a moderator. This officer is chosen by ballot, and acts during the meeting and its several adjournments, as the presiding officer.

TOWN OFFICERS.

Clerk. In every town, a clerk is chosen by ballot, and forthwith sworn by the moderator or a justice of the peace. The clerk is required to record all votes passed at the meetings of the town; to administer the requisite oaths to the other officers, and to keep a record of the same; to record the facts respecting births, marriages, and deaths in the town; to record descriptions of the location of highways; to record the number of votes, and the names of persons voted for at elections of State and county officers, and to make the necessary returns; to issue licenses for dogs; to deliver registers to the school committee; to issue certificates of intentions of marriage; to record mortgages of personal property and assignments of wages.

Selectmen.

Every town elects three, five, seven, or nine Selectmen by ballot. These officers have the general charge of the business of the town; and their duties are many and varied. Some of the more important are the following: they call town meetings; preside, instead of a moderator, at meetings for election of national and State officers, and receive and count the votes; act as a board of health when there is none; appoint men to fill certain minor town offices; lay out town ways; represent the town in its relations to the county and the State, and in suits at law; grant licenses; have charge of the jury-box and drawing jurors; and act as assessors of taxes, and overseers of the poor, if other persons are not specially chosen for the purpose.

Assessors.

Towns may elect three or more Assessors of taxes, and, if deemed expedient, three or more assistant assessors. These officers are required to take an oath to perform their duty impartially. The statutes prescribe minutely what property is liable to taxation, and the mode of apportionment.

Poll-Tax. Every male inhabitant of the Commonwealth above the age of twenty years is liable to a poll-tax, which by law cannot exceed two dollars.

Taxable Property. The property subject to taxation includes all lands and buildings within the State, goods, chattels, money and effects, ships and vessels, money at interest, and debts due the person more than his own indebtedness, stocks and bonds, and income from employment.

Property exempted from Taxation. Some property in the State is exempted from taxation. This includes the property of the United States and of the Commonwealth, the personal property of literary and charitable institutions, houses of religious worship, cemeteries and tombs, the property of agricultural societies, household furniture not exceeding one thousand dollars in value, wearing apparel, and farmers' and mechanics' tools, two thousand dollars of the income from employment, a part of the property of certain widows and unmarried females, young cattle; and the assessors are allowed to exempt the polls and estates of such persons as by reason of age, infirmity, and poverty, they judge unable to contribute fully to the public charges.

Where Taxes are Assessed. The poll-tax is assessed annually upon each person, in the place where he is an inhabitant on the first day of May. Taxes on real estate are assessed in the city or town where the estate lies, to the person who is the owner on the first day of May. In general, taxes on personal estate are assessed to the owner in the city or town where he is an inhabitant on the first day of May, though there are several exceptions to this. The State and county taxes are assessed by the town officers, usually with the town taxes. The amount to be raised for the town is determined by vote at the annual meeting.

Mode of Assessment.

About the 1st of May in each year, the assessors give public notice to the inhabitants, requesting them to bring to the assessors, within a specified time, true lists of their polls and estates not exempted from taxation. Persons bringing such lists are to make oath that they are true. In case any fail to bring the required list, or refuse to be sworn, the assessors are to ascertain, as fully as possible, the kind and amount of taxable property for which these persons are liable. Having completed the inventory of the polls and property subject to taxation, the officers assess the State and county taxes upon the polls. If either of these taxes exceeds one dollar on each poll, the excess must be assessed upon property; and all town and city taxes must be assessed upon property according to law. When the assessment is finished, the assessors make out a list of the names of persons taxed, with a description of their property, and the amount of the tax. This list is sworn to by the assessors as being, according to their best knowledge and belief, a true list of the property; and they affirm that the assessment thereon is full and accurate. This list is given to the collector, with a warrant specifying his duties, and when and to whom he shall pay the money collected. Any person feeling aggrieved by the assessment may petition the assessors for an abatement, which they may grant for satisfactory reasons. If the abatement is refused, and if the person has brought in the required list and taken the required oath, he may appeal to the county commissioners, or to the Superior Court.

Collector of Taxes.

Each town may choose a collector of taxes. If none is chosen, the constable performs the duties. This officer gives bonds to the town for the faithful discharge of his duties. Having received from the assessors the tax-list and the accompanying warrant, it is his duty to collect the taxes. If a tax is not paid within a specified time, the collector may seize the property, or such portion of it as he deems necessary, and, after public notice, may sell it at auction, refunding to the owner whatever is received at the sale above the tax and costs of collection. If a person refuses to pay his tax, and the collector cannot find sufficient property for the purpose, he may take the person, and commit him to prison, to remain until he pays the tax and costs, or until he is released by process of law.

Treasurer.

A Treasurer is chosen annually by ballot, who gives bonds for his fidelity, and whose duty it is to receive and take charge of all sums of money belonging to the town, and pay over the same to the order of the proper officers. He is required to make an annual report to the town, of his receipts and payments.

Constables.

Constables are chosen by ballot. They give bonds to the town, and, having done so, are empowered to serve writs and other legal processes specified by law. They serve warrants issued to them by the selectmen, convey persons to the county jail or house of correction, pursue offenders, and prosecute for the violation of the Sunday laws, and the laws against profane swearing and gaming. In towns having no police force, the constables perform many police duties. They summon persons chosen to various town offices to appear before the town clerk, and take the required oath: they also summon the persons who have been drawn as jurors.

Overseers of the Poor.

Among the beneficent provisions of the Massachusetts statutes is the following: "Every city and town shall relieve and support all poor and indigent persons lawfully settled therein, whenever they stand in need thereof." To carry out this requirement is the business of the Overseers of the Poor,[1] three or more of whom may be chosen by any town annually. If these are not chosen, the selectmen perform their duties. They have the care of all such poor as long as they remain dependent upon the town, and see that they are suitably relieved, supported, and employed. They have the oversight of the town almshouse, employing a keeper, and making the necessary regulations for the care and employment of the persons supported. They represent the town in its dealings with other towns in relation to the settlement and support of paupers.

School Committee.

Each town is required annually to elect by ballot a board of School Committee. The number composing the board is determined by the town, but it must be a multiple of three. The term of service is three years, one third of the board being elected annually. A vacancy in the board is filled by joint vote of the remaining members and the selectmen. The person chosen to fill the vacancy holds office only until the end of the official year, when the town chooses some one for the remainder of the

[1] Women may be elected to this office.

term. This board has the general charge and superintendence of all the public schools in town. It has a secretary, who keeps a permanent record of its proceedings. The school committee selects and contracts with the teachers of the public schools, and personally examines them as to their qualifications to teach and govern; and it may dismiss from employment any teacher whenever it thinks proper. Teachers, before entering upon their duties, must receive a certificate of qualification from the committee, a duplicate of which must be deposited with the selectmen before they are entitled to any pay for services. It is the duty of the committee to visit all the public schools once a month to ascertain their condition and wants. It decides what text-books shall be used in the schools, and makes arrangements for furnishing them to the pupils. Any town may require the committee to choose a superintendent of schools, who, under the direction and control of the committee, shall have the care and supervision of the schools. The school committee is required to make an annual detailed report to the town of the condition of the schools, with such suggestions as to their improvement as it deems proper.

Superintendent of Streets.

In each town the selectmen annually appoint a person to be Superintendent of Streets. He has full charge of all labor and repairs upon streets, bridges, and side-walks, and the care and preservation of shade-trees. If no other provision is made, he also superintends repairs of sewers and drains. He acts under the direction of the selectmen, and may be removed by them. Instead of a Superintendent of Streets, any town may create a board of three road commissioners, chosen for three years by ballot, one retiring annually. This board has the care of the roads and bridges of the town. A town may choose a sewer commissioner and one or more surveyors of highways.

Field-drivers are required to be chosen by all the towns. The number is not specified. Each town is also to maintain one or more sufficient pounds, or places for the enclosure and safe keeping of stray cattle, and annually to appoint a pound-keeper. It is the duty of the field-driver to take swine, sheep, horses, and cattle going at large in the highway without a keeper, and to put them in the pound. It is the duty of the pound-keeper to care for the animals while in his custody, and not to deliver them to the owner until the fees of the officers, and the expense of keeping, have been paid. The field-driver is required to notify the owner of beasts which he has impounded; and, if the owner is not known, to post a description of the beasts in some public place; and, if this is not sufficient, to publish the same in a newspaper. If the owner of animals which have been taken and are held does not pay the charges thereon, the property may be sold at auction, and the expenses deducted from the proceeds.

Field-Drivers.

Another town officer is the fence-viewer, two or more of whom each town must choose. The duty of these men is to settle disputes between the owners of adjoining estates respecting the partition-fences. They serve only on application, and are paid by the person employing them. They decide what portion of a partition-fence each of two parties shall maintain, or divide the expense between them; and, in cases of neglect, they direct proper fences to be erected.

Fence-Viewers.

Surveyors of Lumber.

One or more Surveyors of Lumber are chosen, whose duty it is, when requested to do so by the purchaser or seller, to examine, measure, and mark any lumber brought into the State for sale, or manufactured within the State. Ship-timber, ornamental woods, and building lumber, brought into the State for sale, *must* be surveyed and marked.

Measurers of Wood.

Measurers of Wood are chosen by the town, or appointed by the selectmen. All firewood and bark exposed for sale in a market or upon a cart must be measured by the public measurer.

Sealers of Weights and Measures.

The town at its annual meeting, or the selectmen, must appoint one or more Sealers of Weights and Measures. The State has established as the standard weights and measures those received from the United States Government. These are kept in the office of the treasurer of the Commonwealth. Each county, town, and city is furnished with a complete set of copies of the standard. These are in the custody of the treasurers, but are delivered by them to the sealers. It is the duty of these officers, annually, to notify persons using weights and measures for buying and selling, to bring these to be adjusted and sealed. The sealers are required to go to such large scales and balances as cannot be moved. The statutes forbid the use of weights, measures, and scales which have not been sealed.

Auditors.

Each town is required to choose annually one or more Auditors, who may hold no other town office. It is the duty of these officers to examine the books and accounts of all town officers and committees who are entrusted with the receipt, custody, or expenditure of money. This examination must be made once each year, and may be made once each month. An annual report of the examination is required.

SUMMARY OF TOWN OFFICERS.

Clerk;
Selectmen, three, five, seven, or nine;
Assessors, three or more;
Collector of Taxes;
Treasurer;
Constables, one or more;
Overseers of the Poor, three or more;
School Committee, some multiple of three;
Superintendent of Streets;
Field-Drivers;
Fence-Viewers, two or more;
Surveyors of Lumber, one or more;
Measurers of Wood, one or more;
Sealers of Weights and Measures, one or more;
Auditors, one or more.

The clerk, selectmen, assessors, treasurer, constables, and school committee are required to be elected by ballot; the others, as the town determines. All the officers, except the school committee and the sealers of weights and measures, must be sworn. All may be chosen for terms of three years.

CHAPTER XXIII.

CITIES.

City Charter.

WHEN the population of a town exceeds twelve thousand, and so becomes too large to transact public business in a general town meeting, a different organization may be substituted for the one described in the last chapter. The legislature grants to the people of the town a new act of incorporation, called a city charter. The legislature cannot force a city organization upon any town. The charter must be accepted by a majority of the legal voters at a meeting called for the purpose. Amendments to the charter are also made by the legislature. This instrument gives to the people authority to choose different officers from those prescribed to towns in the general statutes, and to transact local business in a different way; but the general powers and duties of the city organization are the same as those of the towns.

Voting Precincts.

For convenience in election the city is divided into districts called wards, the number of which is specified in the charter. Each of these wards is a voting precinct, if it contains less than five hundred voters. If it contains more than one thousand voters it must, and if it contains more than five hundred it may, be divided into precincts. In each precinct the following officers are appointed by the mayor and aldermen: a warden, a deputy-warden, a clerk, a deputy-clerk, four inspectors, and four deputy-inspectors. These officers are to be appointed equally from the two largest political parties. It is their duty to receive, sort, and count the ballots cast at all elections. The warden has the same duties as the moderator of a town meeting. The clerk keeps a record of the proceedings. The inspectors assist the warden in sorting and counting the ballots. They are all appointed for one year, and are sworn to a faithful discharge of their duties.

City Council.

The entire administration of city affairs is vested in an officer called the Mayor, a board of Aldermen, and in most of the cities, another larger board called the Common Council. The two boards together constitute the City Council.

Election of Officers.

The mayor is elected by the legal voters of the whole city. In most cities the aldermen are chosen by the voters at large, one or more being usually selected from each ward. In some of the cities, each ward elects one or more aldermen. The members of the common council are always elected by the wards. The school committee is usually elected by the wards, though in several cities, beside the ward members are some elected at large. Assessors of taxes are, in some cities, elected by the city council; in others, by the voters. Overseers of the poor are elected in the same two ways in different cities. The city clerk, treasurer, and collector of taxes are elected by joint vote of the two branches of the city council, or by the aldermen when there is no common council. In nearly all the cities, superintendents of streets, engineers of fire departments, a city physician, a city solicitor, and an auditor of accounts are chosen either by joint or concurrent vote of the city council.

City Physician. The duties of the city physician are, to care for the sick paupers and other persons in charge of the city authorities, to prepare annual bills of mortality of the city, to advise the city officers in cases of infectious diseases.

City Solicitor. The duties of the city solicitor are, to draft all legal instruments required in the conduct of city affairs, to act as attorney in all cases at law in which the city is a party, to give legal advice when required by any city officer in the discharge of his duties.

Inferior Officers. A large number of inferior officers are appointed; some by joint vote of the city council, some by concurrent vote, and some by the mayor subject to confirmation by the board of aldermen. Among these are fence-viewers, field-drivers, pound-keepers; surveyors and inspectors of various articles of trade, as wood, lumber, coal, lime, leather, meats, fish, milk; sealers of weights and measures, inspectors of buildings, and commissioners in charge of cemeteries, water-works, and public libraries.

Duties of the Mayor. The mayor is the chief executive officer of the city. It is his duty to see that the laws of the city are enforced, and to supervise the conduct of subordinate officers. He calls special meetings of the city council, and gives such information and makes such recommendations as he deems necessary. He generally presides in the board of aldermen and in convention of the two boards, but has only a casting vote. His salary is fixed by vote of the city council. In cities, the mayor has a veto power similar to that of the governor of the Commonwealth.

The mayor and aldermen together constitute one board, and, in general, have the powers and duties of selectmen. They have exclusive control of police matters, the mayor with the consent of the board of aldermen appointing all constables and police-officers. They issue warrants for ward meetings, and have the care of jury-lists and of drawing jurors. They have the initiative of all business relating to laying out and altering streets, though final action requires the concurrent vote of the other branch. They may, upon the request of a prescribed number of voters, call a general meeting of the voters of the city.

Duties of the Mayor and Aldermen.

Those powers that are exercised by the town in general meetings are, in the cities, exercised by the city council. Measures for raising, appropriating, and borrowing money, the erection of public buildings or other public works, creating public offices, the salaries of officials, regulations to secure public order and safety — all these are determined by concurrent vote of the two branches, in cities having two branches, each having a negative upon the other. In some of the cities, the mayor's approval is also required.

Duties of the City Council.

Those regulations to promote the local welfare, which in the towns are called by-laws, are in the cities called ordinances; and they vary in number and variety with the population of the place. The more dense the population, the more poverty and crime, and the more danger from accident, fire, and infectious diseases. The city ordinances are minute in their requirements respecting the removal of offal and filth; the construction of sewers and drains; the erec-

City Ordinances.

tion and use of buildings; the obstruction of streets by teams, or of sidewalks by ice and snow; the sale of meats, milk, fish, and vegetables. They require the most careful precautions against fires. They punish truancy and vagrancy, because they are the source of crime. They protect public property in parks and cemeteries from mischievous or malicious injury. Any of these ordinances may be annulled by the General Court.

Comparison of City and Town.

In comparing the government of a city with that of a town, we see that the legislative functions are exercised by the city council, instead of by the whole body of voters. The town organization is more democratic than the city, and for this reason adapted only to a small community. The executive functions are performed by the mayor and aldermen, instead of by selectmen. The inferior officers are elected by the city council, instead of by the people. The voters meet in districts for election, instead of in one body.

CHAPTER XXIV.

ELECTIONS AND NOMINATIONS.

THE time and manner of electing State and county officers are prescribed by statute, and are uniform throughout the Commonwealth. The time is the Tuesday next after the first Monday in November.

Time of Election.

The following qualifications entitle a person to vote for officers in the Commonwealth of Massachusetts: —

Qualifications of Voters.

Sex,— male.[1]

Political relation,— citizen of the Commonwealth of Massachusetts.

Age,— twenty-one years or upwards.

Residence,— within the State one year, and within the city or town where he wishes to vote six months, next preceding the election.

Education,— must be able to read the Constitution of the Commonwealth in the English language, and write his name.

There are some exceptions to these requisitions. Paupers, and persons under guardianship, may not vote. The requirement respecting education does not apply to per-

Exceptions.

1 Women having the other necessary qualifications may vote for school-committee.

sons physically disqualified from complying with it, nor to persons who were voters when the requirement was established in 1857, nor to persons who were at that time sixty years old and upwards.

Registry of Voters.

In towns of less than three hundred voters the selectmen and the town clerk constitute a board of registrars of voters; in towns of more than three hundred voters the board is appointed by the selectmen; in cities the board is appointed by the mayor with the approval of the board of aldermen. This board consists of four members. It makes and keeps a record of all persons qualified to vote, including the name, age, birthplace, residence, and occupation. It also prepares lists of qualified voters and posts them in public places as required by law. It is required to be in session at prescribed times to register the names of persons who apply for the purpose, and to correct the lists accordingly. Registration ceases in towns at ten o'clock in the evening of the Saturday last but one preceding an election, and in cities on the twentieth day preceding an election. The board of registrars must be appointed equally from the two largest political parties.

"Australian" System of Voting.

For the election of State and national officers, the ballots are prepared by the Secretary of State, and printed and distributed to local officers at State expense. These ballots contain the names and places of residence of all the candidates for all the offices, with a designation of the party whose principles they represent. There are also blanks for the insertion of other names. At each voting-place are two inspectors, detailed to act as ballot-clerks. These men have a list of the registered voters, and on application to them a person wishing to vote may receive one ballot, his name being then checked on the list. The voter may then enter an enclosure, where are compartments containing materials for marking the ballots. He shows his choice among the candidates by a mark (x) opposite the name. He then folds his ballot and deposits it in the box provided for the purpose, when his name is again checked, this time by the inspectors of election. No one may see him mark his ballot, and he is forbidden to show it before putting it into the box. The object of the *secret* ballot is to prevent bribery and intimidation, that each voter may vote freely and independently. In elections of city officers the mode of voting is the same, the ballots being provided at city expense. In the towns, officers are chosen in a less formal way, each registered voter depositing his ballot containing the names of the persons whom he prefers for the various offices. There are no compartments, no marking of ballots, no injunction of secrecy.

Records and Returns.

The town and city clerks enter in full upon the public records the names of the persons voted for, the number of votes for each, and the title of the office for which each is proposed. Within ten days from the election of State and county officers, the clerks are required to send a sealed copy of this record of the election to the secretary of the Commonwealth.

Certificates.

The secretary transmits these returned copies to the governor and council, who examine them. The governor then issues a summons to the persons chosen to the various executive offices, and to the senators. To the sheriffs, registers of probate, district attorneys, and the clerks of courts, he sends certificates of their election. The persons chosen to the house of representatives receive certificates of election, made out by the clerks of the several towns or cities in the district, who meet for the purpose of examining the records of votes, and ascertaining the result. Duplicate certificates are sent to the secretary of the Commonwealth. The returns of votes for county commissioners are examined by a board of examiners in each county. The commissioners themselves examine the returns for treasurer, and register of deeds.

Official Year. The official year in Massachusetts begins on the first Wednesday in January. On that day, the legislature meets, and the secretary of the Commonwealth lays before the two houses the returns of votes for executive officers. The returns are examined, and the results of the election declared. The officers are then ready to be qualified by taking the required oaths. The term of each officer continues until a successor is elected and qualified.

Removals. The Constitution provides that judicial officers may be removed by the governor with consent of council, upon the request of both houses of the legislature. The members of the general court may be expelled by their respective houses. Executive officers can only be removed by impeachment.

NOMINATIONS.

Under the colonial government of Massachusetts the nomination, as well as the election of officers, was regulated by law. But now the selection of candidates is left to be determined by the various political parties into which the people are divided; and by them the whole matter is systematized.

Each party has a State committee, whose business it is to look after the general interest of the party, and to promote its success. There is also a committee in each county and in each town, city, and ward in the county. Early in the fall of each year, the State committee issues a call for a convention to nominate candidates for the executive offices. This call states the basis of representation in the convention, one delegate being allowed for a specified number of legal voters. Upon receiving this notice, the city and town committees issue calls for caucuses. These are meetings of the voters of the party, for the purpose of choosing delegates to the convention. The local committee is also chosen annually at a caucus.

Committees.

Call of Convention.

Caucus.

The delegates from all the cities and towns meet at the appointed time, and, after organizing, choose by ballot candidates for governor, lieutenant-governor, secretary, treasurer, auditor, and attorney-general. The State committee is also chosen at this time. After the nominations are made, a series of resolutions is usually adopted, setting forth the principles of the party which the nominees are supposed to represent. During the autumn, conventions are held in the counties for the nomination of county officers, and in the councillor and senatorial districts to nominate candidates for the respective offices. To all of these, delegates are sent from the local caucuses.

Nominating Convention.

Representatives to the General Court are nominated by a convention in each district. Each party having made its nominations, the campaign, as it is called, opens. Every effort is made by public meetings, by the newspapers, and by personal

The Campaign.

influence, to secure the greatest number of votes for each candidate; and the work goes on, under the supervision of the various committees, until the day of election.

Objections to the System. This convention system makes it possible for political managers to control the election. The voter, on the day of election, has little room for choice. He must either vote for the nominee of his party or of the opposite party, or throw away his ballot by casting it for some person who has no chance of election. He may like neither of the candidates; and his vote may only indicate his choice of evils. It is now too late for him to protest.

Importance of the Caucus. The place of influence is the caucus. If that is controlled by politicians for selfish purposes, the candidates will be men of the same stamp, and the government will be corrupt. The fate of the nation is decided at the caucuses, not at the elections. If it is a duty of every voter to vote, it is a more imperative duty for him to attend the primary meetings of his party. If he does not do so, he has no right to complain of dishonest or incompetent officials. He must blame himself for his own negligence.

PART IV.

THE CONSTITUTIONAL GOVERNMENT OF THE UNITED STATES.

CHAPTER XXV.

THE HISTORY OF THE UNION BEFORE THE CONSTITUTION.

Tendencies to Separation.

THE brief sketch which we have given of the early history of the thirteen English colonies in America has shown the great diversity that existed, not only in origin, but in the character of the people. This diversity was the cause of mutual jealousies. Local prejudices abounded; and frequently disputes about territory and boundaries brought open hostilities. Though the people were all British subjects, yet only common dangers led them very gradually to see that, as Americans, they had common interests. Colonial union was not accomplished by any one act or succession of acts. It developed, under the pressure of circumstances, as a sentiment in the minds of the people, before it existed as a fact in their history. It was foreshadowed in the New England confederacy, and promoted by the constant aggressions of the French.

Early Colonial Conferences.

As early as 1690, the General Court of Massachusetts, by letters addressed to the other New England colonies and New York, invited them to unite in a meeting of commissioners to consult and determine for their common safety. In this conference four colonies were represented, — Massachusetts,

Plymouth, Connecticut, and New York. They agreed upon measures for raising a joint army, and devised the various plans which were carried into execution during what is known as King William's war. It was a common occurrence for commissioners from several of the colonies to meet to treat with the Indian tribes; and there was frequent official correspondence between them relating to the common defence.

Union favored by two Parties.

The idea of a permanent union was advocated about this time, and various plans were suggested; one by William Penn. Union was favored by two opposite classes. One party desired to promote the interests of the colonies, and strengthen them in their free organization. The other, friends of royalty, wished to check the spirit of freedom by subjecting all to the control of one central authority directed by the crown.

The Albany Convention.

In 1754, by request of the British Government, a convention was held at Albany, consisting of delegates from seven of the colonies. The object of the meeting was twofold: first, to form a treaty of alliance with the chief of the Six Nations; second, to enter into a union, or confederation, with each other for mutual defence. This convention adopted a plan of confederation prepared by Benjamin Franklin. This scheme proposed to leave the government of each colony in its existing form, giving to the local legislatures the power to choose members of a grand council, which should be the legislature of the union. This body was to meet annually, and was to have power to deal in all matters with the Indians, to provide for the common defence, and to levy taxes within the colonies to meet necessary expenses. Its laws were to be submitted to the king, and might be disapproved by him within three years. There was to be a president-general appointed and supported by the crown. He was to nominate military officers, deal in Indian affairs, and execute the laws of the grand council, upon whose acts he was to have a negative. This plan met with little favor from any of the colonies. They were not yet ready for union. It seemed intended, that, when they did unite, it should be as independent States, rather than as subject provinces.

The Colonial Congress.

Ten years later, a long step was taken towards union. The passage of the Stamp Act led the leading patriots in the colonies to see the absolute necessity of a union of all the colonies in resisting arbitrary measures of the British Government. Adams, Otis, and the Warrens, of Massachusetts, from this time onward, were unceasing in their efforts to bring about so desirable a result. The first step was taken by Massachusetts, in calling a general congress, representing the assemblies of all the colonies. This first general colonial congress was held in New York, in October, 1765. It consisted of twenty-eight delegates, from nine of the colonies. Virginia, New Hampshire, Georgia, and North Carolina, though sympathizing with the movement, did not send representatives. The congress adopted a declaration of rights and grievances, an address to the king, and one to the House of Lords, and a petition to the House of Commons. These acts were ratified by the colonial assemblies.

Committees of Correspondence.

This congress, like the conventions that had preceded it, was chosen for a temporary purpose, and, having done its work, dissolved. It required nine years more of British aggression to bring the masses of the people up to the idea of a permanent union. During these years, the union spirit was fostered by the machinery of committees of correspondence, devised by Samuel Adams, and chosen in most of the towns of Massachusetts, and afterward in the other colonies. By means of these, the people of different sections were kept acquainted with each other's views and plans; and every new measure of the government served to draw them closer together.

The Continental Congress.

After the passage of the Boston Port Bill, the desire became general to form another congress; and, in response to a call from Massachusetts, on the 5th of September, 1774, fifty-five delegates from twelve colonies met in Philadelphia, and began the sessions of the famed Continental Congress. Georgia did not send delegates at first, but promised to concur with the other colonies. This body prepared a declaration of rights and grievances, an address to the king, one to the people of Great Britain, and another to the people of the northern provinces.

The Non-Intercourse Association.

But the most important act was the formation by the delegates, for themselves and the colonies they represented, of an association for the non-importation, non-exportation, and non-consumption of British merchandise. The articles of agreement established rules for the government of the people in matters pertaining to the use of imported goods. This has been called "the first enactment of a general law by America," "the commencement of the American Union." The action of this congress was most heartily indorsed by the people throughout the colonies; and either in conventions chosen for the purpose, or by the colonial assemblies, all the colonies but Georgia and New York ratified the articles of the association, and assumed obligations to them as to a *national law*.

Ability of the Congress.

The men who composed this first Continental Congress were the ablest and wisest among the American people. Lord Chatham, in the House of Lords, said of them, "For myself, I must declare and avow, that in all my reading and observation, — and it has been my favorite study: I have read Thucydides, and have studied and admired the master states of the world, — that for solidity of reasoning, force of sagacity, and wisdom of conclusion, under such a complication of circumstances, no nation, or body of men, can stand in preference to the General Congress at Philadelphia."

Union Accomplished.

That the sentiment of union, of nationality, was now complete, is shown by the treatment, in the different colonies, of the plan of conciliation proposed by the British Government. This plan was submitted to each colony separately, in the hope to induce some to make terms with the crown, and so weaken the popular party. But every assembly refused to treat separately with Great Britain, declaring that they should leave the whole matter to the general congress. From this time, the thirteen American colonies were one people. As such, they were represented by the Continental Congress, which met again as a permanent institution in the following May, and continued its sessions from time to time until 1781. It at once showed its national character by assuming the support of the army gathered about Boston, and by appointing Washington commander-in-chief, and still more decidedly by entering into negotiations with foreign nations. Union was now an accomplished fact. But the machinery of government was defective; and, after the Declaration of Independence, the congress began to discuss plans for a more formal confederation.

THE CONFEDERATION.

The Declaration of Independence changed entirely the political character of the American colonies. The people were now independent and sovereign; and as such they proceeded at once to organize themselves in accordance with their changed condition. They adopted, by popular vote, State constitutions based upon the American ideas of local self-government. But, in all, the sphere of State government was limited to its own internal affairs. None of the constitutions made any provisions for intercourse with foreign nations. This external sovereignty the people had already vested in the general congress; and they never withdrew it.

Formation of Confederation.

On the 11th of June, 1776, a committee was appointed by Congress to prepare articles of confederation. This committee reported in July following; but the views and interests of the various colonies were so diverse, and so many vexing questions arose as to the relative authority of the local and general governments, that it was not until November, 1777, that the articles were finally adopted by Congress, and submitted to the States. It was not until March 1, 1781, that Maryland, the last of the colonies, ratified them. On the 2d of March, 1781, the new government went into operation.

The instrument was called "Articles of Confederation and Perpetual Union between the States." The confederacy was styled "The United States of America;" and it was declared to be "a league of friendship," for "common defence," "security of liberties," and "mutual and general welfare." Each State was to retain its sovereignty, freedom, and independence, and every power, jurisdiction, and right not expressly delegated by the articles to the United States Congress. A citizen of any State was to be treated as such by every other State; and full liberty of travel and commerce was guaranteed. Fugitives from justice were to be delivered up.

Nature and Powers of the Union.

The general government had but one department. This was a Congress, to be composed of delegates from the States, chosen in such a manner as the legislatures should direct. No State could have less than two or more than seven members. The delegates were supported by the State, and might be recalled at any time. In the conduct of business in the Congress, each State had one vote, determined by a majority of its delegates. This had been the practice of the Continental Congress. The Congress had sole power respecting peace and war, ambassadors, treaties and alliances, and matters pertaining to the capture and disposal of prizes taken in war. It had also the sole right to fix the value of coin, and the standard of weights and measures, to manage Indian affairs, establish postal communication, appoint land and naval officers, and make rules for the government of the forces and the direction of operations. It was the business of the Congress to ascertain and appropriate the sums of money necessary to meet the public expenses;

Congress.

to borrow money or emit bills on the credit of the United States; to decide upon the number of land forces and the quota of each State, this quota being based upon the number of white inhabitants. The more important of these powers could not be exercised without the consent of nine States.

Executive Business.

The executive business was transacted by committees and officers appointed by the Congress. A committee, consisting of one member from each State, was also appointed to sit during the recess, and execute such of the less important powers of the Congress as might be delegated to it by that body. The States were forbidden to exercise the functions delegated to the Congress.

Finances.

The expenses of the general government were to be defrayed out of a common treasury supplied by the States, each paying to it in proportion to the value of land granted and surveyed within its limits. The taxes for this purpose were to be levied by the authority of the State legislatures, the time being fixed by the Congress.

Every State agreed to comply with the requisitions of the Congress, to inviolably observe all the articles of the confederation, and to make the union perpetual. The articles were not to be altered except by the Congress with the assent of all the State legislatures. The instrument contains no hint of a possibility of voluntary withdrawal by any State.

Defects of the Confederation.

The leading minds of the country foresaw that the government established by these articles would not meet the necessities of the nation. But this was the best that could be obtained at that time. A few years of trial convinced the people of the defects of the confederation. In looking for these defects, we notice first the nature of the union. Out of this grew all other evils. It was called a league of States; and complete internal sovereignty was granted to each of these local organizations.

1. In its Nature.

It followed directly from this, that the Congress had no coercive power. It could not go within the States to deal with individuals; and the States themselves could not be coerced by the ordinary processes of law. Since there was no power to coerce, there was no penalty attached to the enactments of Congress, and therefore no judiciary to apply, and no executive to enforce them. They had not the essential qualities of laws: they were only recommendations. The elements of government are law, penalty, judgment, execution. The confederation was destitute of all these. It was only government in name.

2. No Coercive Power.

A third defective feature was the fact that the power to tax was reserved to the States, and they might and did disregard the levies made by the Congress. The confederation had not power to collect a dollar. Hence it had no credit; for this is based on confidence in the ability of the borrower to pay. If he has no property, and no means of getting any, he will not be trusted. A government without money or credit cannot sustain itself any better than a man can in the same circumstances. Its promises to pay are worthless. For this reason the paper money issued by the Continental Congress during the Revolution rapidly depreciated, until at the close of the war a bushel of it would not buy a breakfast. The evils that resulted from this condition of affairs were many and

3. No Power to Tax.

grievous. The soldiers were unpaid, the army contractors were clamorous for their dues; and, worse than all, thousands of families whose entire wealth had been invested in continental money were suddenly reduced to poverty.

4. No Power to Regulate Commerce.

Another defect in the articles was the withholding from the Congress of the power to regulate commerce. This led to the greatest diversity in the commercial enactments of the several States. Each State adopted a selfish policy, trying to build up its own commerce at the expense of its neighbors. Mutual jealousies and bitterness grew out of this conduct. The Congress could make no commercial treaties with other nations, because it had no power to enforce their provisions upon the citizens of the States.

Recapitulation.

Recapitulating these defects, we find them to be, the nature of the union, the want of coercive power, the absence of a judiciary and a responsible executive, the inability to tax, the consequent loss of credit, and the absence of power to regulate commerce. In consequence of all these, the confederation failed to inspire respect at home and abroad. All parties came to see that it could not meet the requirements of the union, and that every day the union itself was growing weaker. But these very defects were valuable lessons from which the people learned how to build up a more stable government.

CHAPTER XXVI.

THE ORIGIN AND OBJECTS OF THE CONSTITUTION.

Preliminary Measures.

THE commercial troubles, mentioned in the last chapter, led the legislatures of Maryland and Virginia, in 1785, to appoint commissioners to make a compact relative to the navigation of the Potomac River and Chesapeake Bay. The commissioners found that they had too little power, and recommended to their legislatures a convention in which all the States should be represented, and which should devise means to secure uniformity in commercial regulations. Virginia issued a call to all the States; and five of them — New York, New Jersey, Pennsylvania, Delaware, and Virginia — sent commissioners to Annapolis in 1786. They found their powers too limited, and proposed another convention in which delegates from all the States should "take into consideration the situation of the United States," and "devise such further provisions as should appear to them necessary to render the constitution of the federal government adequate to the exigencies of the Union."

The Convention of 1787.

In February, 1787, Congress passed a resolution recommending a convention to meet in Philadelphia in the ensuing May, for the purpose of revising the articles of confederation. All the

States except Rhode Island sent delegates, who met at the appointed time and place. George Washington was chosen president of the convention. It was found impossible to secure the desired end by using the articles of confederation as a basis; and an entirely new constitution was drafted, differing from the old in the nature, form, and powers of the government which it proposed. This draft was discussed and amended, and in its final form adopted by the convention Sept. 17, 1787. It was then submitted to Congress, and by that body transmitted to the legislatures of the States, with a recommendation that it be laid before a convention of delegates chosen for that purpose by the people in each State. Within a year, the Constitution was ratified by conventions in eleven States. North Carolina ratified in 1789, and Rhode Island in 1790. In March, 1789, the new government went into operation.

Ratification.

The ratification was only secured by the most strenuous efforts of the friends of the Constitution. There was hardly a feature of it that escaped criticism; and its most important provisions were subject to opposition on the most diverse grounds. Experience has shown how groundless were most of the fears, and how absurd were many of the objections.

Objections to the Constitution.

The discussions which followed the publication of the Constitution divided the country into two great parties, — the Federalists who advocated, and the Anti-Federalists who opposed, its ratification. Among the men whose influence was most powerful in favor of the new government, were James Madison and Alexander Hamilton. They to-

The Federalist.

gether wrote, and published in a New York newspaper, a series of articles which now constitute one work entitled "The Federalist." Of the eighty-five papers in the work, Mr. Hamilton probably wrote about sixty, Mr. Jay five or six, and Mr. Madison the remainder. They are rich in historical illustrations, and discuss thoroughly and ably the various objections to the new government.

THE OBJECTS OF THE CONSTITUTION.

Preamble.

The objects of the Constitution are stated in the brief preamble: "We, the people of the United States, in order to form a more perfect union, establish justice, insure domestic tranquillity, provide for the common defence, promote the general welfare, and secure the blessings of liberty to ourselves and our posterity, do ordain and establish this Constitution for the United States of America."

1. Union.

The language used in this preamble throws much light upon the nature of the new union. It was to be a "more perfect union" than had previously existed. That union was a league of States, and perhaps as perfect as such a union could be. To improve it, its nature must be changed. Hence, instead of a league of States, a union of people is formed. A *nation* is organized, instead of a *confederation*. The underlying principle of the constitutional government is *national*, not *federal*. The people of the United States is one people. The Constitution is ordained and established by this people, for this people. While the instrument, as we shall see, recognizes the existence of States, and provides for their continuance, it does not derive its authority from them; they are not the original parties to the agreement, nor are they, as States, subjects of the government. The people of the United States by this act constitute one state, whose name is the United States of America.

2. Justice.

While each State had its own judicial tribunals, and aimed to secure justice among its own citizens, the local laws frequently discriminated most unjustly against the citizens of other States. This was especially true of the laws relative to the payment of debts. In the settlement of disputes concerning the property of citizens of foreign nations, there was no uniformity; and the treaties with those nations were persistently violated by local legislation. There was an absolute necessity for some tribunal possessing supreme authority, which should have a national jurisdiction, by which inter-state and international justice should be established.

3. Domestic Tranquillity.

During the period of the confederation, the country was in a most deplorable condition. There was a complete stagnation in business. The States were burdened by heavy war debts; and many of the citizens were bankrupt. Taxes were necessarily heavy, but the poverty of the people made them seem doubly oppressive. In this state of affairs, in 1786, the peace of Massachusetts was disturbed by persons who gathered in large numbers at the various county towns in the western and central parts of the State, to prevent the holding of the courts. These people complained that the government was extravagant and oppressive; that the courts were held in the interests of the rich. They demanded that the taxes should be lightened, and that the suits for debt should be stayed. The tone and actions of these men were so alarming, and their number so formidable, that it became necessary to call out the militia of the State. They were finally dispersed after one or two slight engagements, with the loss of several lives. This disturbance is called Shays' Rebellion, from Daniel Shays, one of the leaders of the insurgents. If some action were not taken by which the public credit could be restored, and the various industries of the people revived, such disturbances were likely to occur at any time and in any locality. Hence the third object of the Constitution was stated to be "to insure domestic tranquillity."

4. Defence.

"To provide for the common defence" had been the leading object in all the various movements towards union. To secure this, the heartiest co-operation of all the States was needed. But, in the present state of affairs, voluntary co-operation could not be hoped for. There must be a central authority competent to inspire confidence at home and respect abroad. The general government must have the power to raise armies, and the power of taxation to support them. Only in this way could the common defence be longer provided for.

5. General Welfare.

All the objects that have been stated would, if attained, have tended "to promote the general welfare;" but there were more direct benefits to be hoped from a national government. Regulating commerce, fostering industries irrespective of sectional interests, carrying on internal improvements, establishing communication between the States, encouraging science — all these it was the object of the Constitution to secure.

The final object of the Constitution is stated to be,

"to secure the blessings of liberty to ourselves and our posterity." Since the settlement of the colonies, their history had been one continual struggle for liberty. This boon they had now acquired. But it needed no peculiar sagacity to foresee that thirteen small sovereign States could not exist side by side, and all retain their independence. Mutual jealousies would provoke hostility; the weaker would become the prey of the stronger; and, thus divided, all might again be brought under the power of some foreign state. History furnishes numerous illustrations of such disasters. To *secure* the blessings of liberty was as necessary as to *acquire* them.

6. Security of Liberty.

While this preamble confers no powers upon the government under the Constitution, it serves to show the scope of its powers, and to throw light upon the interpretation of obscure provisions. We have now to examine the constitution in detail to see how it accomplishes the objects for which the people ordained it.

CHAPTER XXVII.

THE LEGISLATIVE DEPARTMENT.

ALL legislative powers granted by the Constitution are vested in a Congress of the United States, which consists of a Senate and House of Representatives. **Name.**

HOUSE OF REPRESENTATIVES.

The number of members of the first House of Representatives was fixed by the Constitution at sixty-five; but subsequently the number has been determined by Congress, and has changed from time to time as the population of the country has increased. The Constitution provides that the number shall at no time exceed one for every thirty thousand inhabitants. The number of members apportioned on the census of 1900 is three hundred and eighty-six. **Number of Members.**

The representatives are chosen by the people of the several States. The States are divided into congressional districts, in each of which the people elect one representative. But this district system is established by law, not by the Constitution. Any person who, in any State, is entitled by law to vote for members of the larger branch of the legislature, may vote for representative in Congress. **Choice.**

Qualifications of voters are thus determined by the States, not by the general government.

Apportionment.

The representatives are apportioned among the States according to the number of inhabitants, excluding from that number Indians not taxed. When the Constitution was formed, the number of inhabitants on which representation was based was made up by adding to the whole number of free persons those bound to service for a term of years, and three-fifths of the slaves; excluding, as now, Indians not taxed. Since the abolition of slavery, the Constitution has been amended to meet the changed circumstances. This apportionment is made after each decennial census, beginning with 1790. The whole number of people in the United States is divided by the number of representatives, which has been previously fixed by Congress. The quotient is the number of inhabitants entitled to one representative: it is called the ratio of representation. The population of each State is divided by this number; and the quotient is the number of representatives to which the State is entitled. There are remainders, so that the number apportioned to the States is less than the number fixed by Congress. One additional representative is assigned to each of the States having the largest remainders, until the whole number is made up. The Constitution provides that each State shall have at least one representative. If a new State is admitted to the Union between two successive apportionments, it is generally allowed one representative until the next census. The ratio of representation for the present decade is 173,901. Massachusetts has fourteen representatives.

Besides the representatives from the States, provided

for by the Constitution, Congress has by law authorized each organized Territory to send one person, who is called a delegate. These persons sit with the representatives, and take part in the discussions, but have no vote.

Delegates.

The term of service is two years. The official year begins on the 4th of March. As the government was organized under the Constitution in 1789, there is a new house of representatives in March of each odd year. If a vacancy occurs in the representation of any State, it is filled by a new election, ordered by the governor.

Term.

The following are the requisite qualifications of a representative: —

Qualifications.

1. He must be at least twenty-five years of age.
2. He must have been at least seven years a citizen of the United States.
3. When elected, he must be an inhabitant of the State.

The House of Representatives is organized in the same way as the State legislatures. The House elects one of its members as speaker. The clerk, sergeant-at-arms, chaplain, and other officers, are not members.

Officers.

The House of Representatives has two special powers: 1. to present articles of impeachment; 2. to originate all bills for raising revenue, though the Senate may amend these.

Special Powers.

THE SENATE.

The Senate of the United States is composed of two senators from each State. They are chosen by the legislature of the State. The members of each house, on the same day, vote *viva voce* for a senator. On the next day the two houses meet in convention; and if the same person has received a majority of all the votes cast in each house he is declared elected. If no person has received such majorities, then the two houses, sitting as one body, proceed to vote *viva voce;* and, if a majority of both houses is present, the person who receives a majority of the votes cast is declared elected. If there is no choice on the first day, they are required to meet, and take at least one vote each day, until choice is made or the session closes. This method is prescribed by a United States law.

Number and Choice of Members.

The term of service is six years. The first members were arranged in three classes, one-third retiring in two years, one-third in four years, and one-third in six years. By this arrangement one-third of the Senate retires biennially.

Term.

Vacancies.

If a vacancy happens, by resignation or otherwise, and the legislature of the State is not in session, the governor may make a temporary appointment until the next meeting of the legislature, when the vacancy is filled in the usual way. The person so chosen holds office only for the remainder of the term for which his predecessor was elected.

The following are the requisite qualifications of a senator: —

Qualifications.

1. He must be at least thirty years of age.

2. He must have been at least nine years a citizen of the United States.

3. When elected, he must be an inhabitant of the State.

The organization of the Senate is similar to that of the House. The vice-president of the United States is the presiding officer of the Senate; but has no vote, except the house be equally divided. In the absence of the vice-president, a president *pro tempore* performs his functions.

Organization.

The Senate has some peculiar executive functions, which will be noticed in the next chapter. It has also the power to try all impeachments. The details of the trial will be considered separately.

Special Powers.

GENERAL PROVISIONS RESPECTING CONGRESS.

Each house is the judge of the elections, returns, and qualifications of its members. Each house makes its own rules of order, and may punish its members for disorderly conduct, and by vote of two-thirds may expel a member. Members are sometimes publicly reprimanded by the speaker, on vote of the house, for using unparliamentary language, or for other official misconduct. Members of the House of Representatives were expelled in the early part of the war of the Rebellion, for treasonable language and acts.

Control of Membership.

A majority of each house is a quorum; and, in order to secure this, a smaller number have the power to compel the attendance of absent members. Less than a quorum may adjourn from day to day.

Quorum.

Oaths. Each member of Congress is required to take oath to support the Constitution; and, since the war of the Rebellion, this oath has been made more explicit.

Prohibitions. No member of either house can, during the time for which he was elected, be appointed to any civil office under the United States which has been created, or the salary of which has been increased, during his term. No person holding any office under the United States can be a member of either house during his continuance in office.

Sessions. The Constitution requires at least one annual session of Congress, to begin on the first Monday in December, unless a different time be fixed by law. Each Congress[1] usually holds two sessions: one longer, beginning in December of the odd year, and continuing until the next midsummer; a second, shorter, beginning in December of the even year, and continuing until the 4th of March following, when the term of service of all the representatives, and of one-third of the senators, expires. Other sessions are sometimes held, either at times fixed by Congress, or when called by the President. Neither house can, during the session, without the consent of the other, adjourn for more than three days, nor to any other place than that in which the Congress is sitting.

[1] By the phrase, "a Congress," is meant the two branches holding office during any one representative term. Thus the first house of representatives and the senators in office during the first two years formed the first Congress; and each Congress is distinguished by the number of the representative term, dating from March 4, 1789. The Congress whose term began March 4, 1901, was the fifty-seventh.

The compensation of the members of Congress is determined by law, and is paid out of the treasury of the United States. The salary has been increased from time to time. At present the salary of representatives and senators is five thousand dollars a year, with compensation for travelling expenses. The presiding officer of each branch receives eight thousand dollars.

Salary.

The steps in making laws are essentially the same in Congress as in the State legislatures. After passing the two houses, bills are sent to the President. If he approves, he signs: if not, he returns the bill to the house in which it originated, where his objections are recorded, and the bill is again voted upon. If it is approved by two-thirds of each house, it becomes a law. The President has ten days, Sundays excepted, in which to consider the bill. If he does not return it within that time, it becomes a law without his signature, unless Congress adjourns before the expiration of the ten days.

Making Laws.

Veto.

Business is transacted, as in other legislative bodies, by the help of committees. In the house of representatives, the appointment of committees is vested in the Speaker. This is a difficult and delicate task. It is customary to have the two leading political parties represented in each committee nearly in the proportion which they have in the house. The most important committees are, the committee of ways and means, — whose work is to devise means for raising the money necessary to carry on the government, — the committee on appropriations, on commerce, on banks and currency, on the judiciary. The position of chair-

Committees.

man of one of these committees is a most honorable one; and the Speaker must not only seek fitness for the places, but he must fill them with members from different parts of the country, to avoid sectional jealousy. The senate appoints its own committees, the lists being made up by caucuses of the two parties, previously held.

Form of Congress a Compromise.

The form of the legislative department was adopted after much discussion and opposition. The small States demanded equality of representation in both houses: the large States wished it in neither. The federal and national ideas were in conflict. The result was a compromise. The house of representatives embodies the national idea, the members being chosen directly by the people, and the number being proportioned to the population. The senate represents the federal idea, the members being chosen by the legislature, and all the States being equally represented.

CHAPTER XXVIII.

THE EXECUTIVE AND JUDICIAL DEPARTMENTS.

THE PRESIDENT.

ALL executive power is vested in a single officer styled The President of the United States.

Term.

His term of service is four years; and he may be re-elected. The example of Washington in declining a second re-election has practically limited the term of the office to two consecutive terms.

The President is required to have the following qualifications:

Qualifications.

1. He must be a native citizen. 2. He must be at least thirty-five years of age. 3. He must have been for at least fourteen years a resident in the United States.

The manner of choosing a President is as follows: —

Mode of Election.

1. The people of each State choose a body of men called Electors. The number of these is the same as the number of senators and representatives which the State sends to Congress.

Electors.

No senator, or representative, or person holding any office of trust or profit under the United States, can be an elector. A law requires electors to be chosen in all the States on the Tuesday next after the first Monday in November.

Electoral Vote.

2. The electors meet in their respective States, usually in the capital, and vote by ballot for president. The Constitution requires the electors to vote on the same day in all the States; and a law fixes the second Monday in January as the time. The electors make three lists, each containing the names of the persons voted for, and the number of votes for each. These lists are signed by all the electors, and sealed; and a person is appointed by them to carry one list to the president of the senate, at the seat of the national government; another is sent by mail, directed to the same officer; and the third is delivered to the judge of the United States Court for the district in which the electors meet.

Counting the Votes.

3. If a list of votes is not received from a State at the seat of government at the proper time, a messenger is sent for the one in the hands of the district judge. On the second Wednesday in February, the two houses of Congress meet as one body; and the president of the senate opens the certificates. The votes are then counted by tellers appointed for the purpose; and the person, if such there be, having a number of votes equal to a majority of the whole number of electors appointed, is declared elected.

Election by House of Representatives.

4. If no person has such majority, then the representatives proceed at once to choose a president. For this purpose two-thirds of the States must be represented. The voting is by ballot and by States, each State having one vote; and a majority of the States is required for election. The choice of the house must be from the three persons having the highest numbers of electoral votes. The

balloting of the house may continue until the 4th of March ensuing; when, if there has been no choice, the vice-president assumes the duties of president.

The mode of election as above described is contained in an amendment to the Constitution. The original mode, as prescribed by the Constitution, was different. The electors, instead of voting separately for president and vice-president, each voted for two persons, without specifying the office. When the votes were counted, the person having a majority of the votes was declared president; and the person having the next highest number was declared vice-president. If two persons had a majority, and each had the same number of votes, the house of representatives chose between them. Thomas Jefferson was thus chosen. If no one had a majority, the representatives proceeded to choose a president from the five names on the list having the most votes. John Quincy Adams was chosen by the House after the amendment.

Original Mode of Election.

The president may be removed from office by impeachment; and in case of such removal, or death, or resignation, or inability to perform the duties of the office, the Constitution provides that these duties shall devolve upon the vice-president. If neither should be able to perform the duties, Congress has by law declared that one of the heads of the executive departments shall act as president until the disability is removed or a president is elected. The heads of the departments are to succeed in the following order: secretary of state, secretary of treasury, secretary of war, attorney-general, postmaster-general, secretary of navy, secretary of interior. If the first office should be vacant or its incumbent ineligible, the second in order

Vacancy.

would act as president, and so on through the list. To act as president these officers must be eligible as president under the constitution.

Oath of Office. At noon on the fourth day of March, the chief justice of the supreme court of the United States administers to the president elect the oath of office required by the Constitution: "I do solemnly swear that I will faithfully execute the office of President of the United States, and will to the best of my ability preserve, protect, and defend the Constitution of the United States." This ceremony is the inauguration of the president; and it is customary for him to deliver an address appropriate to the occasion.

Salary. The compensation of the president is fixed by Congress; but the Constitution requires that it shall not be increased or diminished during his term of service, and that he shall not receive within that period any other emolument from the United States, or from any of the States. During the first term of Washington's administration, the salary was fixed at twenty-five thousand dollars a year; and it remained unchanged until 1873, when it was raised to fifty thousand dollars a year. In addition to this, the executive mansion, called the White House, is furnished to the president rent free, together with its furniture, fuel, lights, care of grounds, etc.

THE VICE-PRESIDENT.

Election. When the electors vote for president, they also vote by distinct ballots for a vice-president. They make similar lists of the persons voted for, and send them with the others; and the votes are counted at the same time. The person having a majority of the electoral votes is declared vice-president. If no person has such majority, the senate proceeds at once to choose a vice-president from the two persons having the highest number of votes.

Duties.

The qualifications requisite for the vice-president are the same as for the president; and he is chosen for the same term. He is not strictly connected with the executive department, having no executive functions unless in case of a vacancy in the office of president, when he assumes the duties of that position. He is more closely connected with the legislative department, being president of the senate, though he has no vote unless the senate be equally divided. The salary of the vice-president is fixed by Congress, and is now eight thousand dollars a year.

Nomination.

The choice of president and vice-president by electors, and not directly by the people, would seem to preclude a previous nomination. This was doubtless the intention of the framers of the Constitution, to avoid the excitement of a popular election. But in this respect the purposes of the fathers have been defeated. Each of the political parties of the country has a national, as well as a State, committee. In the summer preceding the choice of electors, these committees issue calls for national conventions composed of delegates from the States. These delegates are chosen at State conventions, which consist of delegates chosen in town and ward caucuses. At the national conventions, candidates are nominated for the office of president and vice-president; and their friends come before the people with their claims, just as if the people were to vote directly for them. At subsequent State conventions, persons are nominated for electors, pledged to vote for the party candidates. For these persons the people vote, with the understanding that by so doing they are expressing their choice for president. All that the electors have to do is to record their votes for the persons previously agreed upon. The electoral voting is therefore only a form. If the candidate should die between the time of the choice of electors, and the day for them to vote, the responsibility of choice would fall more directly upon them.

JUDICIAL DEPARTMENT.

Supreme Court. The Constitution vests judicial power in one supreme court, and such inferior courts as Congress shall from time to time establish. The Supreme Court of the United States consists of one chief justice and eight associate justices. It holds an annual term in Washington, beginning on the second Monday in October.

Circuit Courts. The United States has been divided by Congress into nine judicial circuits, in each of which are two justices. Each justice of the supreme court holds a circuit court with the assistance of one of the circuit justices.

District Courts. These circuits are divided into districts, in each of which is a judge, a clerk, a marshal, and an attorney. Some of the larger States are divided into two or three districts; each of the others forms one district. The duties of the marshal are similar to those of the sheriff in the State courts.

Circuit Court of Appeals. In each circuit is a Circuit Court of Appeals consisting of three judges. The supreme court justice for the circuit, the circuit judges and the district judges within the circuit are competent to compose this court. A term of this court is held annually in each circuit. Its business is to exercise appellate jurisdiction over certain prescribed cases from the district and circuit courts.

Court of Claims.

Besides the courts of justice that have been described, there is a Court of Claims, consisting of five justices. The business of this court is to examine all claims against the government for the payment of money about which there is dispute, and to make such awards as the court deems just. As a sovereign state cannot be sued in an ordinary court, justice requires that some such provision should be made for the benefit of the public creditors.

Appointment and Salary of Judges.

All the judges are appointed by the president, with the advice and consent of the senate. They hold their office during good behavior, and may be removed by impeachment and subsequent conviction. Their compensation is fixed by law; but the Constitution provides that it shall not be diminished during their continuance in office. The marshals and district attorneys are also appointed by the president.

CHAPTER XXIX.

THE POWERS OF CONGRESS.

1. RESPECTING FINANCE.

Power of Taxation.

THE superiority of the constitutional government over the confederation is nowhere more apparent than in the extensive powers given to Congress for raising money. The grant is as follows: "Congress shall have power to *lay* and *collect* taxes, duties, imposts, and excises, to pay the debts and provide for the common defence and general welfare of the United States." The four words used are intended to cover all forms of taxation. A tax is "a contribution imposed by government on individuals for the service of the state." Duties, in a restricted sense, are taxes upon articles imported or exported. Imposts are the same as duties. Excises are taxes upon articles manufactured or produced for home consumption.

Direct Taxes.

The Constitution divides taxes into two classes, direct and indirect, and prescribes different modes of apportionment. Direct taxes include poll-taxes, — that is, taxes upon the person of the contributors, — and taxes on land, houses, and other real estate. These must be apportioned as representatives are; that is, according to the population of the several States. This provision was a compromise between the slaveholding and non-slaveholding States. The former wished all the slaves counted in the representative population: the latter wished none of them counted. The controversy was settled by counting three-fifths of them both for representation and for taxation. Direct taxes have very rarely been levied by the government of the United States.

Indirect taxes include duties, imposts, and excises. These are required to be uniform throughout the country. Duties upon exports are prohibited. Duties upon imports are of two kinds. *Specific* duties are proportioned to the *quantity* of the article imported; *ad valorem* duties are proportioned to the market value of the article in the country from which it comes, as shown by an invoice accompanying it. A duty of a dollar a yard on silk would be specific; a duty of forty per cent on silk would be *ad valorem*.

Duties.

Congress prescribes the rate of duties to be paid on different articles of merchandise, and the mode of collection. A schedule of dutiable goods, with the rate upon each, is called a *tariff*.

Tariff.

Officers are appointed to inspect all merchandise, to assess the duties upon it, and to collect these. All duties are paid by the importer. For convenience in collection, custom-houses are established at different places on the seacoast, on the navigable rivers, and on the boundary-line between the States and the Dominion of Canada.

Collection of Duties.

During the war of the Rebellion, and the war with Spain, excise duties were levied upon a large number of articles of home production and use; but most of them have since been withdrawn. Taxes of this kind are still levied upon the manufacture of distilled and fermented liquors, of tobacco, and some other articles. Some stamp duties are also levied. These taxes are collected by Internal Revenue officers.

In time of peace, the duties upon imports have been sufficient to meet the expenses of the government; but, to meet extraordinary expenses, Congress has the power to borrow money on the credit of the United States. Congress by law determines the amount to be borrowed, the kind of securities to be given, the rate of interest to be paid, and the time and place of payment of principal and interest. The money is actually borrowed by the secretary of the treasury. Under this provision of the Constitution, Congress authorized the issue of United States notes, payable on demand, without interest, and made them legal tender, that is, lawful money for the payment of debts.

Power to Borrow Money.

Congress has not only the power to provide for a revenue, but the complete control of all expenditures. No money can be drawn from the treasury but in consequence of appropriations made by law; and a regular statement of all receipts and expenditures is required to be published from time to time.

Expenditures.

2. RESPECTING COMMERCE AND COMMERCIAL INTERESTS.

The Constitution gives to Congress power to regulate commerce with foreign nations, and among the several States, and with the Indian tribes.

Under this grant Congress declares what vessels are entitled to protection as American, by what process protection may be secured, at what ports vessels may land cargoes, what rules shall govern the entering and leaving ports. It makes rules for the government of seamen on board of Ameri-

Regulation of Commerce.

can vessels, provides for administering justice to seamen through its courts, and sends consuls to all foreign ports to look after the commercial interests of American citizens. It surveys the coasts, clears harbors and rivers from obstructions, builds breakwaters, erects lighthouses and buoys, and enacts laws respecting pilotage, quarantine, and wrecking.

Promotion of Commercial Interests.

Besides the power to regulate commerce, Congress has other powers which closely concern commercial interests. These are, the power to coin money, to fix the value of American and foreign coins, to fix the standard of weights and measures, to provide for the punishment of counterfeiting the securities and current coin of the United States, and to establish uniform laws on the subject of bankruptcies throughout the United States.

Coining Money.

For coining money, mints are established at various places. The principal one is at Philadelphia; and there are branches at San Francisco; Carson City, Nev.; and Denver, Col. There are assay offices at New York; Charlotte, N.C.; and Boise City, Idaho. Gold and silver bullion is received at either of these places in amount not less than one hundred dollars in value. This is assayed,—that is, tested to ascertain the relative amount of pure metal in it; and the depositor receives for it its value either in coin or in stamped bars, less a small charge for assaying, melting, and coining. The mint and branches are in charge of persons appointed by the president. Congress determines what coins shall be issued, and the standard fineness of each, regulates the charges for coining, and makes all rules for the conduct of the business.

Although Congress has the power to fix the standard of weights and measures for the country, it has never exercised the power. It has adopted the English units for the use of the officers of the government in the custom-houses, and the Troy pound for the mints, and has furnished copies of these to the States, but has not made their use obligatory. There is still considerable diversity in different sections of the country. Congress has also legalized the use of the metric system.

Weights and Measures.

The object of bankrupt laws is to free debtors from all their obligations on giving up their property to their creditors. When the relation of debtor and creditor is held by citizens of different States, it is desirable that the laws regulating their relation should be uniform, or great injustice might be done, and the commerce between the States checked. This uniformity can only be secured by the action of Congress.

Bankrupt Laws.

3. RESPECTING NATURALIZATION.

Congress has the power to establish a uniform rule of naturalization. As the citizens of one State have all the rights of citizens in every other State, it is necessary that the qualifications for citizenship should be the same in all. The process of naturalization consists of two steps. The first is the declaration of intention to become a citizen of the United States. This must be made on oath before a circuit or district court of the United States; or before a State court of record having common law jurisdiction, a clerk, and a seal. This declaration is recorded, and a certificate given to the person.

Declaration of Intention.

At least two years must elapse before the second step, — the oath of allegiance. The person must prove by witness upon oath, that he has resided in the United States at least five years, and in the State in which he wishes to be naturalized at least one year; and that during this time he has borne a good moral character, and has been well disposed toward the Constitution and government. He then makes a written declaration, and supports it by oath, that he renounces allegiance to all foreign powers, and especially the one to which he has been subject, and that he will support the Constitution of the United States. A certificate of citizenship is then given him by the court.

Oath of Allegiance.

If the applicant was under eighteen years of age when he came to this country, the declaration of intention is dispensed with, but the five years of residence must be proved. A soldier who has served in the United States army and been honorably discharged, may become a citizen, after a residence of one year, on taking the oath of allegiance. The wife and minor children, if living in the country, become citizens by the naturalization of the husband and father.

Special Cases.

4. RESPECTING POSTAL COMMUNICATION.

Congress has the power "to establish post-offices and post-roads." This includes all that is necessary to secure prompt delivery of the mails in any part of the country. The ordinary routes of travel, highways and railroads, are adopted by the government as post-roads. Congress declares by law what matter may be transported through the mails and at what rates, fixes the salaries of all officers connected with the service, and prescribes how contracts shall be made for carrying the mails, and for furnishing the necessary articles for the department. The postal money-order system has also been established by Congress, under this provision of the Constitution.

5. RESPECTING PATENTS AND COPYRIGHTS.

Congress has the power "to promote the progress of science and the useful arts by securing for limited times to authors and inventors the exclusive right to their respective writings and discoveries."

Patent. A patent is a written instrument by which the government secures to an inventor the exclusive right to manufacture and sell his invention. The invention may be an art, a machine, a manufacture, or a composition of matter, or any new and useful improvement thereon. The patent is issued for a term of seventeen years.

Copyright. A copyright is the exclusive privilege granted by government to print, publish, and sell copies of writings or drawings. Copyrights are issued to residents of the United States or of such foreign nations as grant corresponding privileges. They cover books, maps, charts, musical compositions, prints, cuts, and engravings, and the representation of dramatic compositions. The copyright is issued by the librarian of Congress, and is valid for a term of twenty-eight years. At the end of that time, the author or his heirs may secure an extension of the right for fourteen years.

6. RESPECTING THE ADMINISTRATION OF JUSTICE.

The Constitution provides for a supreme court, but gives to Congress power to constitute inferior tribunals. Under this power the circuit and district courts, and the court of claims, have been established, and the modes of performing their functions regulated.

Congress has certain other powers which necessarily grow out of the sovereignty of the United States.

Piracy. One of these is, "to define and punish piracies and felonies committed on the high seas, and offences against the law of nations." The term "high seas" means the unenclosed waters of the ocean, and also those waters on the seacoast which are without the boundary of low-water mark. By the law of nations, piracy is defined as a robbery or forcible depredation on the high seas, without lawful authority, in the spirit of universal hostility. Congress declared that murder and robbery on the high seas, or any offence which if committed on land would be punishable with death, shall be considered piracy and felony. The slave-trade has also been declared to be piracy. Piracy is punishable with death.

Treason. The power is also given to Congress to declare the punishment of treason; but the Constitution defines the crime, and limits the penalty. Treason against the United States consists "only in levying war against them, or in adhering to their enemies, giving them aid and comfort." It is further declared that "no person shall be convicted of treason unless on the testimony of two witnesses to the same overt act, or on confession in open court." The student of English history will recall the gross injustice perpetrated during the reigns of the Tudors and Stuarts by calling the most trivial offences treason, and will see the wisdom and prudence of those who guarded against such oppression in our own country. Congress has made treason punishable with death. The punishment by the common law of England was most barbarous; and the convicted person could neither inherit estates, nor retain those already possessed, nor transmit them to any heir. He also forfeited all personal property. But the Constitution of the United States does not allow the guilt of the traitor to be visited upon his children.

7. RESPECTING WAR.

Congress has the power "to declare war, grant letters of marque and reprisal, and make rules concerning captures on land and water." A letter of marque and reprisal is a commission granted by the government to a private individual to take property of a foreign state, or of the citizens or subjects of such state, as a reparation for injury committed by such state, or by its citizens or subjects.

Letter of Marque.

Congress has power to raise and support armies, and to provide and maintain a navy, and to make rules for the government and regulation of the land and naval forces. In the exercise of this power, Congress determines what number of troops shall be maintained in each branch of military service; the manner of organizing and disciplining them; the number, rank, and pay of officers; the way in which the army shall be supplied. It establishes armories for making, and arsenals for storing arms. It has made careful surveys of the territory of the United States for the construction of army maps. It provides

United States Army.

for the care of the national cemeteries, where the bodies of those who have died in their country's service find a last resting-place. It has also established and maintained a military academy at West Point for the education of army officers. The army, in time of peace, is scattered over the United States and its island possessions, doing garrison duty in the forts on the coast, protecting the frontier settlements from hostile natives, or making explorations and surveys.

United States Navy.

Congress determines of what the navy shall consist, and how it shall be organized and officered. It maintains navy-yards for the construction and repair of vessels; and an academy at Annapolis, Md., for the education of naval officers. In time of peace, a part of the vessels are at the navy-yards; and the others are stationed in the various waters of the globe, to protect the interests of the United States and the persons and property of her citizens. Ocean surveys are made, to aid in the construction of charts.

Militia.

Besides the power to support the regular army, Congress has the power to provide for calling out the militia to execute the laws of the Union, suppress insurrection, and repel invasion. In the exercise of this power, Congress has by law conferred upon the president the power to call forth the militia for the purposes specified in the Constitution; and the supreme court has decided that the president is the sole judge of the necessity of issuing the call. Congress also provides for organizing, arming, and disciplining the militia, and for governing such portion of them as may be employed in the service of the United States. Each State officers and trains its own militia, according to the regulations prescribed by Congress.

8. RESPECTING THE TERRITORY AND PROPERTY OF THE UNITED STATES.

Seat of Government. The Constitution gives to Congress the power to exercise "exclusive legislation in all cases whatsoever" over the District of Columbia, and over all places purchased by the government for its own use, as for forts, navy-yards, &c. The District of Columbia was originally a tract of land ten miles square, lying on both sides of the Potomac River, ceded to the United States by Maryland and Virginia. In 1846 the part south of the river was given back to Virginia. As this district is not a part of any State, its inhabitants are not represented in Congress, nor in the choice of president. Congress once gave charters to the cities of Washington and Georgetown; later Congress established a government similar to that of the western Territories; now the affairs of the District are in the hands of three commissioners appointed by the president.

All purchases of land by the United States, for the erection of public buildings or works, must be made with the consent of the legislature of the State in which the land is situated.

Territory. Congress also has the power to dispose of, and make all needful rules and regulations respecting, the territory or other property belonging to the United States. The territory of the United States has been obtained in various ways,—from the individual States by cession, from foreign nations by purchase or by war, from the Indians by purchase, and, as in the cases of Texas and Hawaii, by direct annexation.

Cession by States. The territory granted to several of the colonies by their charters extended to the Pacific Ocean; and after the Revolution these States claimed this land as far west as the Mississippi. The other States denied the justice of the claim, and refused to ratify the articles of confederation unless the unoccupied territory were given up to Congress, to be held for the benefit of all the States. After much discussion, the States of Massachusetts, Connecticut, New York, Pennsylvania, Virginia, the Carolinas, and Georgia, gave up the title to the unoccupied Western land.

Ordinance of 1787. The country north of the Ohio River was called the Northwest Territory. In 1787 Congress passed a famous Ordinance to provide for its government. The right of taxation was asserted, all civil rights were guaranteed, slavery was prohibited, and the declaration made that not less than three nor more than five new States should be formed from the territory, and admitted to the Union on equal terms with the original States.

Louisiana and Florida. France had originally claimed the territory west of the Alleghany Mountains, but in 1763 had given up all east of the Mississippi River. In 1803 the United States by treaty with France purchased the territory south of the thirty-first parallel of latitude, between the Perdido and Mississippi Rivers, and all between the latter river and Mexico. This was divided into the Territory of Orleans, and the District of Louisiana. In 1819 Florida was purchased of Spain. **Texas.** In 1845 Texas, which had previously withdrawn its allegiance from Mexico, and had fought to maintain its independence, at its own request was annexed to the United States. This was considered an act of hostility by Mexico; and the Mexican war followed. This was closed by a treaty in 1848; by which Mexico, for a sum of money, ceded New Mexico and California to the United States. In 1867 the territory of Alaska was purchased of Russia.

California and Alaska.

In 1898 the Hawaiian Islands were annexed to the United States on the request of the inhabitants. In the same year, by the treaty of peace with Spain, Porto Rico, the Philippine Islands, and the island of Guam were ceded to the United States.

Extinction of Indian Rights.

Most of the territory acquired by the earlier cessions and purchase was occupied by Indian tribes. In order to open the country to white settlers, the various tribes were compelled to give up their right of occupancy. To those east of the Mississippi River, land was granted in what is now the Indian Territory; and they were removed thither. The western tribes have gradually been compelled to give up their roving habits, and confine themselves to reservations set apart by Congress.

Disposal of Territory.

Congress, in the exercise of the right to dispose of territory, has had surveys of it made, and has provided for selling it to actual settlers. It has also given it to discharged soldiers, and has made extensive grants to railroad corporations.

Organized Territories.

From time to time, as the population has increased, portions of this territory have been organized for government. The act of Congrėss by which a Territory is organized has the same relation as a constitution in a State government. It fixes the qualification of voters; establishes a legislative department of two branches chosen by the people;

provides for the appointment of a governor, a secretary, and judicial officers, by the President of the United States; determines the relations of the departments; and limits the powers of the government. Thus the principle of local self-government on which the republic rests is respected; but the people, not being inhabitants of a State, have no voice in the general government. As has been stated in a previous chapter, the interests of the people are represented in Congress by a delegate, who may participate in debate, but cannot vote.

Admission of States.

Congress has the power to admit new States into the Union. Two modes of procedure have been followed at different times. Usually the people of a Territory form a State constitution, and submit it to Congress with a petition for admission to the Union. If the government proposed is republican in form, Congress may pass an act of admission. Sometimes Congress takes the first step by passing an enabling act. This allows the people to form a State constitution at a certain time, and authorizes the president to issue a proclamation recognizing the new State if the government is republican in form.

Enabling Acts.

The following States have been admitted:

Vermont, claimed by New Hampshire and New York,	**admitted**	**1791.**
Kentucky, ceded by Virginia,	"	**1792.**
Tennessee, ceded by North Carolina,	"	**1796.**
Ohio, a part of the North-West Territory,	"	**1803.**
Louisiana, acquired from France,	"	**1812.**
Indiana, a part of the North-West Territory,	"	**1816.**
Mississippi, ceded by South Carolina and Georgia,	"	**1817.**
Illinois, a part of the North-West Territory,		**1818.**
Alabama, ceded by South Carolina and Georgia,	"	**1819.**
Maine, set off from Massachusetts,	"	**1820.**
Missouri, acquired from France,	"	**1821.**

Arkansas, acquired from France,	**admitted**	**1836.**
Michigan, a part of the North-West Territory,	**“**	**1837.**
Florida, acquired from Spain,	**“**	**1845.**
Texas, a revolted province of Mexico,	**“**	**1845.**
Iowa, acquired from France,	**“**	**1846.**
Wisconsin, a part of the North-West Territory,	**“**	**1848.**
California, acquired from Mexico,		**1850.**
Minnesota, chiefly acquired from France,	**“**	**1858.**
Oregon, acquired by exploration and settlement,	**“**	**1859.**
Kansas, acquired from France,		**1861.**
West Virginia, a part of Virginia,	**“**	**1863.**
Nevada, acquired from Mexico,	**“**	**1864.**
Nebraska, acquired from France,		**1867.**
Colorado, acquired from France and Mexico,	**“**	**1876.**
North Dakota, acquired from France,	**“**	**1889.**
South Dakota, acquired from France,	**“**	**1889.**
Washington, acquired with Oregon,	**“**	**1889.**
Montana, part from France and part with Oregon,	**“**	**1889.**
Idaho, acquired with Oregon,		**1890.**
Wyoming, acquired from France,	**“**	**1890.**
Utah, acquired from Mexico,	**“**	**1896.**

9. RESPECTING AMENDMENTS TO THE CONSTITUTION.

How Proposed. Amendments may be proposed in either of two ways: first, by Congress, two-thirds of both houses agreeing; second, by a convention for the purpose, called by Congress on application of the legislatures of two-thirds of the States.

How Ratified. These amendments may become valid as parts of the Constitution by being ratified in either of two ways: first, by the legislatures of three-fourths of the States; second, by conventions in three-fourths of the States. Congress may determine which of these two modes shall be used.

Fifteen amendments have been ratified. The absence of any bill of rights in the Constitution excited the jealousy of the people of some of the States; and they urged the immediate adoption of amendments to supply the omission. Accordingly ten amendments were finally ratified by three-fourths of the States in 1791. Eight of these guaranteed the following rights: religious freedom, and freedom of speech and of the press; the right of assembly and petition; the right to keep and bear arms; exemption from quartering soldiers; security from unlawful search and seizure; prompt and impartial justice, and trial by jury; exemption from excessive bail, and from cruel and unusual punishments.

Subject of First Eight Amendments.

The *ninth* amendment declares that the enumeration of the above rights does not imply that others may be violated. The *tenth* reserves to the States or to the people all rights not delegated to the general government. The *eleventh*, ratified in 1798, relates to the judicial power of the United States.

Ninth, Tenth, and Eleventh.

The *twelfth*, ratified in 1804, was occasioned by the contest in the house of representatives which resulted in the election of Thomas Jefferson as president. It prescribes the manner of electing the president and vice-president. The *thirteenth*, ratified in 1865, abolished and prohibited slavery within the United States.

Twelfth and Thirteenth.

The *fourteenth*, ratified in 1868, guarantees political and civil rights to all persons born or naturalized in the United States; changes the rule of apportionment of representatives and direct taxes, to adapt it to a wholly free population; excludes from office under the United States and in the States those rebels who have violated a previous oath of allegiance, but gives to two-thirds of Congress the power to remove this disability; establishes the validity of

Fourteenth and Fifteenth.

the public debt of the United States; forbids the payment by the United States or by any State of any debt incurred in aid of rebellion, or any claim for emancipated slaves; gives to Congress power to enforce the provisions of the amendment by legislation. The *fifteenth*, ratified in 1870, guarantees the right of suffrage to freedmen, and gives to Congress power to enforce the act by legislation.

10. RESPECTING IMPEACHMENT.

Who may be Impeached. By the United States Constitution, the persons who may be impeached are the president, vice-president, and all civil officers of the United States. The term "civil officers" includes all executive and judicial officers of the national government, except those of the army and navy. The members of Congress are not considered United States officers. Civil officers of the States are liable to impeachment by the State legislatures.

Impeachable Offences. The offences for which the United States officers may be impeached are treason, bribery, and other high crimes and misdemeanors. Treason is defined by the Constitution itself; and the other offences are determined according to the principles of parliamentary usage and the common law. In the impeachment of Andrew Johnson, in 1868, the offences charged were the unlawful removal from office of the secretary of war, the appointment of another person to the same office, and the forcible attempt to obtain possession of the war department. These were called high crimes and misdemeanors.

The Constitution gives to the house of representatives the sole power of impeachment. The steps in the process are as follows: 1. A resolution to impeach, naming the person and his office and the offence. 2. The appointment of a committee, who appear before the senate, and, in the name of the house of representatives and the people of the United States, make the impeachment, and demand that the accused be summoned to answer the charges. 3. The appointment of a committee to prepare articles of impeachment. 4. The appointment of a committee to act for the house of representatives in the trial.

Mode of Impeachment.

The senate has the sole power to try impeachments. When sitting for that purpose, the members are required to be on oath or affirmation. When the president of the United States is tried, the chief justice of the supreme court presides. The senate establishes rules to govern its procedure. The whole house of representatives appears before the senate, and the managers present the articles of impeachment. A day is fixed for the trial, and then the proceedings follow as in a court of justice. After the evidence has been presented, and the arguments of the managers and of the defendant's council have been made, each senator is required to answer "Guilty," or "Not guilty," to each of the articles. The Constitution requires for conviction the concurrence of two-thirds of the senators present.

The Trial.

The Constitution provides that "judgment in cases of impeachment shall not extend further than to removal from office, and disqualification to hold any office of honor, trust, or profit under the United States; but the party convicted shall nevertheless be liable and subject to indictment, trial, judgment and punishment, according to law."

Judgment.

CHAPTER XXX.

THE POWERS AND DUTIES OF THE PRESIDENT.

1. AS COMMANDER-IN-CHIEF.

THE president is commander-in-chief of the army and navy of the United States, and of the militia of the States when in the actual service of the United States. In the exercise of this power, he appoints and removes officers, assigns their stations and duties, and directs the movements of the forces.

2. RESPECTING PARDONS.

He has power to grant reprieves and pardons for offences against the United States, except in cases of impeachment. A reprieve is the withdrawing of a sentence for an interval of time, thereby delaying execution.

3. RESPECTING TREATIES.

Definition of Treaty.

He has power, by and with the advice and consent of the senate, to make treaties, provided two-thirds of the senators present concur. A treaty is a compact between two or more independent nations, with a view to the public welfare. The principal subjects of treaties are peace, alliance, territory, boundaries, the settle-

Subjects.

ment of claims, redress of grievances, commerce, navigation, naturalization, and the giving-up of fugitives from justice. Treaties on the last subject are called "extradition treaties."

Formation. Treaties are usually made by agents representing the two governments, the agent of the United States being under the direction of the president. The papers are then laid before the senate, and discussed, where the treaty may be amended, accepted, or rejected. Any amendment must be accepted by the president and by the other government. As the Constitution declares that treaties, as well as the Constitution itself, are the supreme law of the land, the making of treaties is both legislative and executive business: hence the propriety of investing the senate with a share of the power.

4. RESPECTING APPOINTMENTS.

Extent of Power. The president is required to nominate, and, by and with the advice and consent of the senate, to appoint, ambassadors, other public ministers and consuls, judges of the supreme court, and all other officers of the United States whose appointment is not otherwise provided for in the Constitution, and which are established by law. But Congress has the power to vest the appointment of such inferior officers as it thinks proper in the president alone, in the courts of law, or in the heads of departments.

Process. The filling of an office by the president includes four steps: a nomination in writing by the president, a vote to confirm by the senate, the appointment by the president, and the issuing of a commission signed by the president, and sealed with the seal of the United States.

Removals.

The power of removal from office has until recently been supposed to be wholly in the hands of the president; but now a law requires the consent of the senate to removals, as well as appointments. During a recess of the senate, the president may suspend an officer, except a judge of a United States Court, until the end of the next session of the senate, and may appoint a person to fill the temporary vacancy. But, within thirty days after the commencement of the next session of Congress, he must nominate a person for permanent appointment.

Public Ministers.

The president has the power to appoint ambassadors and other public ministers. A Minister is a person sent by a government to represent it in the transaction of business with another government. The term includes officers of various grades. They are called diplomatic agents. It is customary for civilized nations to send representatives to all those foreign nations with whom they desire to maintain friendly intercourse. These officers usually live at the capital of the country to which they are sent. They are supported by their own government, and report to it all matters that concern its interests. Through them business is transacted and courtesies are exchanged. The United States sends ministers with the following titles: minister-plenipotentiary and envoy-extraordinary, minister-resident, and *chargé-d'affaires*. The Constitution requires the president to receive ambassadors and foreign ministers.

The president also appoints consuls. A consul is a commercial agent appointed by a government to reside in a foreign country, and attend to the commercial interests of his nation. He is not a diplomatic agent, but must receive a permit, called an exequatur, from the government to which he is sent, before he can exercise the functions of his office. This permit may be revoked at any time. The business of the consul is very miscellaneous, including receiving declarations made by seamen or others respecting American commerce, administering on the estates of American citizens dying within their consulate without legal representatives, taking charge of stranded American vessels in the absence of interested parties, settling disputes between masters of vessels and the crews, providing for destitute seamen, and sending them to the United States at the public expense. Consuls are paid by salary or by fees. Both are fixed by Congress.

Consuls.

Duties of.

Among the officers whose appointment is by law vested in the president, are the chief officers of the various executive departments, the judges of the various United States courts, district-attorneys and marshals, executive and judicial territorial officers, some postmasters, the more important customs and excise officers, and officers of the army and navy.

Appointments by Law.

The senate may not be in session when a vacancy occurs in an office subject to the appointment of the president; and delay might damage public interests. The president has the power to fill all such vacancies by issuing commissions to expire at the end of the next session of the senate. During the session, it is expected that he will nominate a person for permanent appointment.

Vacancies during Recess.

5. RESPECTING MESSAGES.

The president is required to give to Congress, from time to time, information of the state of the Union, and to recommend such measures as he may judge necessary and expedient. Accordingly, at the opening of each annual session of Congress, he sends a message embodying his opinions and suggestions, accompanied by detailed reports of all branches of the executive service. These department reports contain a vast amount of information respecting the state of the country, its resources, and the progress of their development. The president also sends messages during the sessions, either in answer to calls for information, or at his own pleasure.

EXECUTIVE DEPARTMENTS.

Besides these special duties that have been considered, the president, as the chief executive officer, is required to see that all laws are faithfully executed. This work necessitates the employment of a large number of subordinate officers, and a careful distribution of functions. All the executive business is distributed among eight departments constituted by acts of Congress. The chief officers are: Secretary of State, Secretary of the Treasury, Secretary of War, Secretary of the Navy, Secretary of the Interior, Postmaster-General, Attorney-General, Secretary of Agriculture. These officers constitute the president's cabinet. The Constitution gives him the right to require their opinion in writing upon any subject relating to the duties of their respective offices; but he is not bound to follow their advice, nor is their consent

Cabinet.

required to any executive measure. The cabinet is not a limiting body, and in this respect differs from the executive council in some of the State governments.

DEPARTMENT OF STATE.

The functions of this department are of two kinds; those relating to domestic affairs, and those relating to the foreign relations of the government. The department has the custody of the seal of the United States, and affixes it to all state documents, with the signature of the secretary. It has the keeping of the laws of the United States, and promulgates them. Through this department the president corresponds with and instructs the consuls and diplomatic agents of the government, negotiates with foreign nations, and receives communications from their agents. Passports — that is, certificates of citizenship — are issued by this department to persons needing them for the purpose of foreign travel.

TREASURY DEPARTMENT.

This department has charge of executive business connected with the finances of the government. It prepares plans for the management of the public revenue, and the improvement of the public credit; makes estimates of the revenue and expenditures, and suggests ways to increase the former, and diminish the latter; receives and disburses all moneys coming to the government; superintends the collection of the revenue. The secretary of the treasury is the agent of the government in borrowing money; and the various securities issued are prepared under his direction. This department also has charge of the mints of the United States, of the coast survey, and of the erection and maintenance of light-houses and other safe-guards for navigation. It attends to the execution of all laws relating to commerce and navigation.

WAR DEPARTMENT.

Through this department the president superintends all business relating to the military forces of the United States. It has charge of the army rolls and registers, of military equipments and supplies, of the transportation, pay, and subsistence of the troops; of military hospitals, arsenals, and armories; of the military academy and of military surveys. Through it all orders are issued, and to it reports are made by the officers in the different branches of the service. It also administers military justice.

NAVY DEPARTMENT.

This department has the general charge of the naval force of the United States. It superintends the purchase, building, and repair of vessels; has the care of all navy-yards and docks; provides for the equipment of vessels and crews, and for the clothing, subsistence, health, and pay of officers and men; issues all orders, and receives reports; has charge of the naval academy, and of scientific expeditions to foreign countries.

POST-OFFICE DEPARTMENT.

Through this department all laws respecting the postal system of the country are executed. It establishes post-offices; selects post routes; makes contracts for postal supplies, and for carrying the mails; appoints most of the postmasters, directs all, and receives reports from all; provides and distributes stamps, envelopes, and postal cards; has charge of the money-order system.

The postmaster-general has the power to conclude postal conventions, as they are called, by which the postal communication with foreign nations is regulated.

DEPARTMENT OF THE INTERIOR.

The business of this department is more miscellaneous than that of any other. It has the general charge and superintendence of public lands and public buildings, of pensions, of patents, of Indian affairs, of the census, of mines, of the bureau of education, which collects and disseminates through the country information respecting public education. Each of these divisions is in charge of a commissioner.

DEPARTMENT OF JUSTICE.

At the head of this department is the Attorney-General. He conducts suits in the supreme court in which the United States is a party, and gives legal advice, when requested, to the president and Congress and heads of departments. The subordinate officers are called solicitors, and have charge of legal matters growing out of the business of the several departments.

DEPARTMENT OF AGRICULTURE.

This department collects and publishes information respecting the various branches of agriculture. It seeks to discover new and improved varieties of vegetable products, and distributes seeds of these over the country. It maintains experiment stations for testing the adaptability of the soil and climate of the United States to the productions of foreign countries. It maintains the signal service for the preparation and publication of weather reports.

JUDICIAL POWER OF THE UNITED STATES.

Extent of Jurisdiction.

The Constitution says that the judicial power shall extend to all cases in law and equity arising under the Constitution, the laws of the United States, and treaties made under the authority of the United States. This includes civil and criminal cases.

Law and Equity.

The phrase "law and equity" refers to two distinct kinds of judicial procedure. The first includes all cases that can be settled by the direct application of statutes or the principles of the common law. Equity jurisdiction is intended to reach a large class of cases for which the common-law courts furnish no remedy. The two differ materially in the mode of proof used, and the modes of affording remedy.

Classes of Cases.

Three classes of cases are spoken of: first, those whose settlement depends upon an interpretation of some provision of the Constitution of the United States; second, those which arise from violation of some law of Congress; third, those which arise from violation of some treaty stipulation between the United States and a foreign nation.

Division of Jurisdiction.

While all cases arising in the three classes just mentioned come within the jurisdiction of the courts of the United States, the Constitution has restricted certain kinds of cases to the supreme court, leaving others to the inferior courts, or to be begun in them and finished in the supreme court.

The supreme court has original jurisdiction in two classes of cases only, — those affecting ambassadors, other public ministers, and consuls; and those in which a State is a party. The latter include controversies between two or more States; between a State, and citizens of another State; between a State, and foreign nations, citizens, or subjects; between the citizens of a State, and foreign nations, citizens, or subjects. The eleventh amendment prohibits any suit against a State either by a citizen of another State, or by a citizen or subject of a foreign nation.

Original Jurisdiction of Supreme Court.

The supreme court has appellate jurisdiction both as to law and fact, with such exceptions and under such regulations as Congress shall make, in all cases of admiralty and maritime jurisdiction; in controversies in which the United States is a party; in controversies between citizens of different States; in controversies between citizens of the same State claiming lands under grants of different States.

Appellate Jurisdiction.

Admiralty and maritime jurisdiction includes all suits originating on the high seas, such as those concerning captures by naval forces in time of war, and those growing out of the relations between the owners, officers, and crews of vessels. Of these cases the district and circuit courts have original jurisdiction; but they may be carried to the supreme court for final adjustment.

Admiralty and Maritime Cases.

The supreme court may not only re-examine cases from the inferior courts of the United States, but also from the State courts in cases which involve the interpretation of the Constitution or laws of the United States, or of treaties made under them.

CHAPTER XXXI.

PROVISIONS RESPECTING STATES.

PROHIBITIONS UPON THE STATES.

Concerning Foreign Relations.

THE States are absolutely forbidden by the Constitution to enter into any treaty, alliance, or confederation; or to grant letters of marque and reprisal; they are also forbidden to keep troops or ships of war in time of peace, without the consent of Congress; nor may they without such consent enter into any agreement or compact with another State or foreign power, or engage in war, unless actually invaded, or in such imminent danger as will not admit of delay. The States, as such, have no relation to foreign powers. They assumed this as a fundamental principle of their Union, when they refused to treat separately with Great Britain just before the war for independence. During the war, the Continental Congress represented the United States in their intercourse with other nations. Next, the same powers were vested in the Congress of the confederation; and now the principle is embodied in the Constitution. If each State were free to engage in war, and to negotiate privately with foreign governments, there would be no security for the permanence of the Union, or for the continuance of the liberties of the people. The States must stand or fall together.

The States are forbidden to coin money, to emit bills of credit, to make any thing but gold and silver coin a tender in payment of debts. They are also forbidden to lay any duty of tonnage without the consent of Congress; nor may they lay duties on imports or exports except for special purposes, and under the control of Congress. It will be remembered that the immediate cause which led to the formation of the Constitution was the trouble arising from State legislation respecting commerce. Inequality of taxation of imports produced ill feeling between the States, and checked the commercial prosperity of all. Hence the propriety of giving to the general government exclusive power in this direction. Tonnage duties — that is, charges upon vessels in proportion to their carrying capacity — are forbidden for the same reason. These duties are not now levied by Congress. The general government, too, has exclusive control of the currency. Corporations within the States, as banks, have been allowed to issue bills of credit, that is, notes designed to circulate as money; but these were not legal tender, and the holders might at any time demand gold or silver coin for them.

Concerning Commerce and Commercial Interests.

The States are forbidden to pass any law impairing the obligation of contracts. In the days of the Roman republic, the State repeatedly made general laws for the relief of debtors, freeing them entirely or partly from their obligations. Such laws, and all involving the same principle, are forbidden. No State may pass any bill of attainder, or *ex post facto* law. Congress is also forbidden to pass such laws. The phrase, "bill of attainder," refers to those features of English law by which persons convicted of

Concerning Private Rights.

treason suffer forfeiture of property, and lose the power to transmit to their descendants, so that the children suffer with the parent. An *ex post facto* law is a law made to punish acts previously committed, and which were not punishable, or not punishable in the same manner, by any preceding law.

Concerning Freedmen.

The fourteenth and fifteenth amendments to the Constitution lay certain prohibitions upon the States, designed especially to protect the colored people who have become citizens by the abolition of slavery. No State may make or enforce any law which shall abridge the privileges or immunities of citizens of the United States; nor may any State deprive any person of life, liberty, or property without due process of law, nor deny to any person within its jurisdiction the equal protection of its laws. No State may deny or abridge the right of any citizen of the United States to vote, on account of race, color, or previous condition of servitude.

PROTECTION OF STATE RIGHTS.

In the clause giving to Congress power to admit new States into the Union, it is declared that no new State may be formed within the jurisdiction of another State, nor any State be formed by the junction of two or more States or parts of States, without the consent of the legislatures of the States concerned, as well as of Congress. By this provision, the States secure their continued existence as distinct individuals. But it makes division possible, as in the separation of Maine from Massachusetts, and of West Virginia from Virginia. When the Constitution was formed, the small States were induced to accept it by giving them equal power in the senate with the large ones. To insure the safety of these States, it is provided, that no amendment shall ever be made by which this equal suffrage shall be taken away from any State without its consent. To prevent inequality in the treatment of the States by the general government, it is provided, that no tax or duty may be laid on articles exported from any State; no preference may be given by any regulation of commerce or revenue to the ports of one State over those of another; nor may vessels engaged in commerce between the States be made to pay the usual charges for entrance and departure to which vessels engaged in foreign commerce are subject.

RELATION OF STATES TO EACH OTHER.

1. Public Acts.

The preservation of the Union depends upon the mutual good feeling existing among the States. Nothing but complete equality can prevent jealousies and quarrels. Any assumption of superiority by any State would speedily provoke a spirit hostile to union. The Constitution guards against this by two or three declarations. First, every State must give full faith and credit to the public acts, records, and judicial proceedings of every other State. It cannot question the authority under which they are made; and it must give them full weight as precedents for judgment.

2. Citizenship.

The citizens of each State are entitled to all the privileges and immunities of citizens in every other State. Thus the unity of the people is promoted. Any person who can claim protection of person and property, transact business, vote, and hold office, in one State, may do all these in any other

State, without those conditions and limitations to which aliens might be subjected.

3. Fugitives from Justice. Any person charged with crime in one State, and escaping to another, must be delivered up on demand of the executive of the State from which he has fled. There is nothing that compels an independent nation to deliver up criminals who have taken refuge within its territory. Mention has already been made of the extradition treaties by which the United States has agreed with most of the leading nations for a mutual giving-up of fugitives from justice. If criminals could escape justice by passing from one State of the Union to another, there would be an end to justice in these days of easy communication; and this would be another fruitful source of mutual ill feeling.

Fugitives from Service. There is another provision in this connection, which shows the spirit of concession and compromise which actuated the people at the time of the adoption of the Constitution. The Constitution requires that persons held to service or labor under the laws of one State, and escaping into another, shall not be released from such service; but shall be delivered up to the party claiming the service. Slaves escaping from their masters into a non-slaveholding State could not become free thereby, but were liable, if discovered, to be sent back to their servitude. Though this was repugnant to the feelings of the people of some of the States, they accepted what seemed at the time a lesser evil, for the sake of securing the union they so much needed. It is a significant fact, that the word "*slave*" is nowhere used in the Constitution as originally adopted. While they tolerated the system, the framers of the Constitution had too much regard for consistency, to use the word in a document based on the principles of liberty and justice.

PROVISIONS TO PROTECT PRIVATE RIGHTS.

Habeas Corpus.

The chief safeguard of the people against oppression by the national government is contained in the provision that the privilege of the writ of *habeas corpus* shall not be suspended, unless, in cases of rebellion or invasion, the public safety may require it. The Constitution does not declare who shall be the judge of the necessity of suspending the privilege. In 1863 Congress authorized the president to suspend the privilege of the writ throughout the whole or any part of the United States, whenever in his judgment the public safety might require it. Accordingly it was, by proclamation, suspended in some of the States. But, when the emergency had passed, the right was promptly restored: military rule ceased; municipal law became again supreme, and free to act through the ordinary channels of judicial procedure. This, more than the successful prosecution of the war, was the grand triumph of the government; for, though it may be easy for a government to acquire power, it is not so easy to give it up.

Titles of Nobility.

The Declaration of Independence had stated as a self-evident truth, that all men are created equal. Any artificial division of the people into classes would be contrary to the fundamental principle of the government. Hence the Constitution declares that no title of nobility shall be granted by the United States or by any State. The Constitution also forbids any officer of the United States accepting any present, emolument, office, or title, of any kind whatever, from any king, prince, or foreign state without the consent of Congress. Presents have been made by foreign sovereigns to some of the presidents of the United States; but they have been received officially rather than personally, and are preserved as public property at the seat of government. Congress frequently grants permission to officers to accept gifts from foreign governments.

Trial by Jury.

Another private right that has always been dear to the American people is trial by jury. This is guaranteed by the Constitution itself in criminal cases; and by one of the amendments it is also secured in civil suits when the value in controversy exceeds twenty dollars. The trial is to be held in the State and district where the crime is committed. If not committed in any State, Congress by law determines where the trial shall be held.

Other Rights.

The people of the States, in forming their own constitutions, were careful to provide for all those civil and political rights for which their fathers had struggled in England, and which had been denied them by the British Government. They knew their worth because they knew what they had cost. When the Constitution was presented to them for ratification, without any declaration of these rights, they naturally hesitated, lest they should by their own act create a power that might oppress them. Hence, with their ratification, they presented articles of amendment to supply the defect. These have been noticed in a preceding section.

CHAPTER XXXII.

RELATION OF NATIONAL AND STATE GOVERNMENTS.

Source of Authority.

In the first part of this book it was said, that a state is a whole body of people; that a government is a part of that whole body; that authority to govern is in the state; that this authority is delegated to the government by the state, under conditions and limitations; that the form of the government, and the extent of its powers, are determined by the state; that the state may withdraw its grant of powers in part or wholly, and may delegate again to the same organization or to a new one. These are fundamental principles. In considering the relative authority of the national and state governments, we have to inquire for the people by whom this authority is delegated in each case, and notice their condition before these governments were organized.

Previous to independence, the people of the thirteen English colonies in America held two distinct political relations, — one national, the other local. They all alike belonged to the British nation: its authority, as vested in the king and parliament, was supreme. This relation they held in common. As subjects of Great Britain they were one people.

In another respect they were distinct. That the

functions of local government should be exercised directly by the people most concerned, had always been a cherished idea of the Anglo-Saxon people. In accordance with this idea, the people founding the different colonies had claimed the right of local self-government. The king had so far yielded to this claim as to establish separate organizations, in which the people had more or less power. Thus the people of the colonies were one in their relation to the king, and separate in their local organizations.

During the war for independence, these two relations of oneness and diversity continued, but with this change. The people of the different colonies created permanent organizations for local government, by forming their several State constitutions. The one people of all the colonies established the Continental Congress for such general purposes as seemed necessary, but made at first no complete and permanent organization. As soon as more pressing necessities had been met, they established the confederation as a national government, leaving the local organizations as they were. But they found by short experience, that they had given to the national government too little power, and had left to the local governments too much. Hence the new organization under the Constitution.

The Constitution was made by the same people that formed the confederation. They were one under British rule, one in the war for independence, one under the confederation, and the same one under the Constitution. The government organized by the Constitution received its authority from this one people. It was optional with this people to give up its oneness, to establish no national government, to separate itself into thirteen distinct and independent states, each with all the powers of such. It was also optional to vest all the functions in the national government, giving to it the power to provide for local administration. The first course would have been political suicide; the second would have been to throw away what had been a sacred birthright of their fathers, cherished through a history of a thousand years. They chose neither of these two courses, but organized a national government for national purposes, and allowed the local governments to exist with purely local functions. This idea is expressed in the article which says, "The powers not delegated to the United States by the Constitution, nor prohibited by it to the States, are reserved to the States respectively, or to the people."

The national government, therefore, receives its authority from the whole people of all the States. The State governments exercise what authority the same people has suffered them to retain.

Functions of Each.

The relation of the national and State governments to each other is further shown in the nature of the functions of each. So long as the American people were a part of the British nation, they held no relations to foreign nations. France knew them only as British subjects; and if she had declarations of war to make, or treaties of peace to negotiate, she dealt with the government of Great Britain. She went to headquarters.

But when, at the beginning of the revolution, the Continental Congress addressed the people of Great Britain in the name of the American people, and uttered the Declaration of Independence in the name of the people of the united colonies, France recognized a new nation;

not Massachusetts, nor Virginia, but the American people. The States as such have never sought to be known by foreign nations, but have always been merged in the one people of the United States.

Hence the national government possesses all those functions which grow out of international relations. War and peace, commerce and navigation, all intercourse with other nations — these are wholly and exclusively in the hands of the national government. They were not withdrawn from the State governments. The State governments had never possessed them, and had never claimed them. They were powers wrested from Great Britain by the blood and treasure of the one American people for itself, and not by or for the individual States as such.

The care and disposal of the unoccupied territory of the colonies is another function of the national government, resting on the same basis as those just mentioned. This territory had been acquired by the sacrifices of the whole people; and for this reason they claimed it.

Beside these functions growing out of external relations, the national government has to do with every thing which concerns the nation as a whole; such as the coining of money, the maintenance of postal communication, the issuing of patents. Superadded to all these it has the grand attribute of sovereignty, — unlimited power of taxation. This it exercises not through the state governments, as formerly, but directly, by its own officers, it brings its authority to bear upon the whole people. The national purse gives efficacy to the national sword; and thus two objects of the Constitution are attained, — the common defence, and domestic tranquillity.

A glance at the functions left for the State governments to exercise shows them to be purely local, as they have always been. Their object is to secure personal rights, to provide for the safety and happiness of the individuals of the community, to protect men from their neighbors. Public education, public health, public morals, the detection and punishment of crime, care of local industries and interests — these are some of the subjects over which the State governments have absolute control. The people resisted all attempts of the British Government to interfere with these functions. They never delegated them to any of the national organizations. If the time ever comes when the people do not look with jealousy upon any attempt to centralize these functions, and resist steadfastly all tendencies in this direction, that will be the time of the nation's greatest peril. Guizot says, "The preponderance of local liberties belongs to the infancy of societies. Civilization incessantly tends to carry power still higher. But frequently also, as it ascends, power forgets its origin and final destiny; it forgets that it was founded to maintain all rights, to respect all liberties; and, meeting with no further obstacle from the energy of local liberties, it becomes transformed into despotism." In our effort to maintain the wholeness of the nation, we must avoid weakening this "energy of local liberties." To preserve both in their just relation, is the care of American citizens, and the mission of American statesmen.

National Supremacy.

It might be inferred, from the source of its authority and the nature of its functions, that the national government would be supreme within its sphere. It must be this, or nothing. But this supremacy is declared forcibly in the Constitution itself. "This Constitution, and the laws of the United States which shall be made in pursuance thereof, and all treaties made or which shall be made under the authority of the United States, shall be the supreme law of the land; and the judges in every State shall be bound thereby: any thing in the constitution or laws of any State to the contrary notwithstanding." No local body of law-makers can set aside any expression of the will of the whole people. More than this: the representatives of the States in Congress, the members of the State legislatures, and all executive and judicial officers of the States, are bound by oath or affirmation to support the Constitution of the United States. In the exercise of their several functions, they are to maintain and strengthen the authority of the national government, as well as to preserve the local liberties. There need be no conflict between the national and the State authority; there ought to be none. But, if there should be, the supreme obligation of every citizen, as well as of every officer, is apparent. His highest allegiance is due to the government of the nation as much as if there were no local organizations.

This view of the meaning and force of the Constitution of the United States has been established only after many years of discussion, and finally by force in the Civil War.

In 1798 the States of Virginia and Kentucky, through their legislatures, adopted Resolutions to the effect that the powers of the federal government were limited to the grants specifically made in the instrument of the compact, that whenever the general government assumed undelegated powers, its acts were void and of no force, and that the States had a right to interpose and protect themselves. The States themselves were to be the judges of the constitutionality of the acts of the general government.

In 1814, when the people of the New England States were greatly disturbed over the commercial policy of Jefferson and Madison, many of them gave voice to similar opinions in the famous Hartford convention.

In 1832 South Carolina, aggrieved by the passage of successive protective tariff acts by Congress, declared these acts null and void, and threatened to secede if they were enforced.

Finally, in 1861, the Southern States, carrying out this extreme state-rights doctrine, seceded from the Union. The failure of their effort to disrupt the Union placed the authority of the Constitution of the United States on an impregnable basis. No one now believes that there is anywhere in the history or Constitution of the nation or of the States any provision for a peaceable dissolution of the Union. That can never be anything but an act of violence.

National Protection.

The national government, as well as the whole people, is pledged to maintain the authority of the State governments. The Constitution requires the United States to guarantee to every State a republican form of government, and to protect each from invasion and domestic insurrection. Just what is meant by a republican form of government is not stated; but probably the form of the national government was considered republican. The two chief characteristics of such a government are, that it is *from* the people, and *by* the people; that is, the Constitution is ordained by a majority of the people, and the government is actually administered by persons chosen by the majority in a constitutional way. If by fraud or violence the power in any State should be usurped by an individual, or by a faction, it would be the duty of the national government to furnish to the majority of the people all needed assistance in regaining their rightful authority.

If the government of the State cannot maintain itself, the legislature, or, if it is not in session, the executive, may apply to the national government for aid. If Congress should not be in session, the president would be required to judge of the emergency, and to take such measures as he might think best. At different times the United States has been called upon thus to protect the State governments from domestic violence.

This is one of the most delicate and dangerous duties of the national executive, especially if the disturbance has arisen from the conflict of political parties. There is a jealousy of national interference in State affairs, that within certain limits is healthful; but beyond these limits it would leave the people of the States at the mercy of any demagogue who could acquire a temporary power. But the right and the duty of the national government are unmistakable. Whenever any portion of the people of any State are unjustly deprived of their political rights, the whole people of the Union are bound to reinstate them. The safety of the whole Republic requires the republicanism of every part.

But this does not imply that the national government shall interfere in every political quarrel by which the quiet of a State may be disturbed. This would belittle its character, and weaken its influence. The people of the States should be left to settle these disputes for themselves until the local authority is exhausted, and the general good requires national interference.

APPENDIX.

DECLARATION OF INDEPENDENCE AND CONSTITUTION OF THE UNITED STATES.

APPENDIX.

THE DECLARATION OF INDEPENDENCE.

A DECLARATION BY THE REPRESENTATIVES OF THE UNITED STATES OF AMERICA, IN CONGRESS ASSEMBLED.

When, in the course of human events, it becomes necessary for one people to dissolve the political bands which have connected them with another, and to assume, among the powers of the earth, the separate and equal station to which the laws of nature and of nature's God entitle them, a decent respect to the opinions of mankind requires that they should declare the causes which impel them to the separation.

We hold these truths to be self-evident. that all men are created equal; that they are endowed by their Creator with certain unalienable rights; that among these are life, liberty, and the pursuit of happiness; that, to secure these rights, governments are instituted among men, deriving their just powers from the consent of the governed; that, whenever any form of government becomes destructive of these ends, it is the right of the people to alter or to abolish it, and to institute a new government, laying its foundation on such principles, and organizing its powers in such form, as to them shall seem most likely to effect their safety and happiness. Prudence, indeed, will dictate that governments long established should not be changed for light and transient causes; and accordingly all experience hath shown that mankind are more disposed to suffer, while evils are sufferable, than to right themselves by abolishing the forms to which they are accustomed. But when a long train of abuses and usurpations, pursuing invariably the same object, evinces a design to reduce them under absolute despotism, it is their right, it is their duty, to throw off such government, and to provide new guards for their future security. Such has been the patient sufferance of these colonies; and such is now the necessity which constrains them to alter their former systems of government. The history of the present king of Great Britain is a history of repeated injuries and usurpations, all having, in direct object, the establishment of an absolute tyranny over these States. To prove this, let facts be submitted to a candid world: —

He has refused his assent to laws the most wholesome and necessary for the public good.

He has forbidden his governors to pass laws of immediate and pressing importance, unless suspended in their operations till his assent should be obtained; and, when so suspended, he has utterly neglected to attend to them.

He has refused to pass other laws for the accommodation of large districts of people, unless those people would relinquish the right of representation in the legislature; a right inestimable to them, and formidable to tyrants only.

He has called together legislative bodies at places unusual, uncomfortable, and distant from the depository of their public records, for the sole purpose of fatiguing them into compliance with his measures.

He has dissolved representative houses repeatedly, for opposing, with manly firmness, his invasions on the rights of the people.

He has refused, for a long time after such dissolutions, to cause others to be elected; whereby the legislative powers, incapable of annihilation, have returned to the people at large for their exercise; the State remaining, in the mean time, exposed to all the dangers of invasion from without, and convulsions within.

He has endeavored to prevent the population of these States; for that purpose, obstructing the laws for the naturalization of foreigners, refusing to pass others to encourage their migration hither, and raising the conditions of new appropriations of lands.

He has obstructed the administration of justice, by refusing his assent to laws for establishing judiciary powers.

He has made judges dependent on his will alone for the tenure of their offices, and the amount and payment of their salaries.

He has erected a multitude of new offices, and sent hither swarms of officers to harass our people, and eat out their substance.

He has kept among us, in times of peace, standing armies, without the consent of our legislature.

He has affected to render the military independent of, and superior to, the civil power.

He has combined, with others, to subject us to a jurisdiction foreign to our constitution, and unacknowledged by our laws; giving his assent to their acts of pretended legislation :—

For quartering large bodies of armed troops among us;

For protecting them, by a mock trial, from punishment for any murders which they should commit on the inhabitants of these States;

For cutting off our trade with all parts of the world;

For imposing taxes on us without our consent;

For depriving us, in many cases, of the benefits of trial by jury;

For transporting us beyond seas to be tried for pretended offences;

For abolishing the free system of English laws in a neighboring province, establishing therein an arbitrary government, and enlarging its boundaries, so as to render it at once an example and fit instrument for introducing the same absolute rule into these colonies;

For taking away our charters, abolishing our most valuable laws, and altering, fundamentally, the forms of our governments;

For suspending our own legislatures, and declaring themselves invested with power to legislate for us in all cases whatsoever.

He has abdicated government here, by declaring us out of his protection, and waging war against us.

He has plundered our seas, ravaged our coasts, burnt our towns, and destroyed the lives of our people.

He is, at this time, transporting large armies of foreign mercenaries to complete the works of death, desolation, and tyranny already begun with circumstances of cruelty and perfidy scarcely paralleled in the most barbarous ages, and totally unworthy the head of a civilized nation.

He has constrained our fellow-citizens, taken captive on the high seas, to bear arms against their country, to become the executioners of their friends and brethren, or to fall themselves by their hands.

He has excited domestic insurrection amongst us, and has endeavored to bring on the inhabitants of our frontiers the merciless Indian savages, whose known rule of warfare is an undistinguished destruction of all ages, sexes, and conditions.

In every stage of these oppressions, we have petitioned for redress, in the most humble terms; our repeated petitions have been answered only by repeated injury. A prince whose character is thus marked by every act which may define a tyrant is unfit to be the ruler of a free people.

Nor have we been wanting in attention to our British brethren.

We have warned them, from time to time, of attempts made by their legislature to extend an unwarrantable jurisdiction over us. We have reminded them of the circumstances of our emigration and settlement here. We have appealed to their native justice and magnanimity; and we have conjured them, by the ties of our common kindred, to disavow these usurpations, which would inevitably interrupt our connections and correspondence. They, too, have been deaf to the voice of justice and of consanguinity. We must therefore acquiesce in the necessity which denounces our separation, and hold them, as we hold the rest of mankind, enemies in war, in peace, friends.

We, therefore, the representatives of the UNITED STATES OF AMERICA, in GENERAL CONGRESS assembled, appealing to the Supreme Judge of the world for the rectitude of our intentions, do, in the name and by the authority of the good people of these colonies, solemnly publish and declare, That these United Colonies are, and of right ought to be, *free and independent States;* that they are absolved from all allegiance to the British crown; and that all political connection between them and the state of Great Britain is and ought to be totally dissolved; and that, as FREE AND INDEPENDENT STATES, they have full power to levy war, conclude peace, contract alliances, establish commerce, and to do all other acts and things which INDEPENDENT STATES may of right do. And for the support of this declaration, with a firm reliance on the protection of DIVINE PROVIDENCE, we mutually pledge to each other, our lives, our fortunes, and our sacred honor.

THE CONSTITUTION OF THE UNITED STATES.

WE, the people of the United States, in order to form a more perfect union, establish justice, insure domestic tranquillity, provide for the common defence, promote the general welfare, and secure the blessings of liberty to ourselves and our posterity, do ordain and establish this CONSTITUTION FOR THE UNITED STATES OF AMERICA.

ARTICLE I.

SECTION 1. All legislative powers herein granted shall be vested in a Congress of the United States, which shall consist of a senate, and house of representatives.

SECT. 2. The house of representatives shall be composed of members chosen every second year by the people of the several States; and the electors in each State shall have the qualifications requisite for electors of the most numerous branch of the State legislature.

No person shall be a representative who shall not have attained to the age of twenty-five years, and been seven years a citizen of the United States, and who shall not, when elected, be an inhabitant of that State in which he shall be chosen.

Representatives and direct taxes shall be apportioned among the several States which may be included within this Union, according to their respective numbers, which shall be determined by adding to the whole number of free persons, including those bound to service for a term of years, and excluding Indians not taxed, three-fifths of all other persons. The actual enumeration shall be made within three years after the first meeting of the Congress of the United States, and within every subsequent term of ten years, in such manner as they shall by law direct. The number of representatives shall not exceed one for every thirty thousand; but each State shall have at least one representative; and, until such enumeration shall be made, the State of New Hampshire shall be entitled to choose three, Massachusetts eight, Rhode Island and Providence Plantations one, Connecticut five, New York six, New Jersey four, Pennsylvania eight, Delaware one, Maryland six, Virginia ten, North Carolina five, South Carolina five, and Georgia three.

When vacancies happen in the representation from any State, the executive authority thereof shall issue writs of election to fill such vacancies.

The house of representatives shall choose their speaker and other officers, and shall have the sole power of impeachment.

SECT. 3. The senate of the United States shall be composed of two senators from each State, chosen by the legislature thereof, for six years; and each senator shall have one vote.

Immediately after they shall be assembled in consequence of the first election, they shall be divided, as equally as may be, into three classes. The seats of the senators of the first class shall be vacated at the expiration of the second year; of the second class, at the expiration of the fourth year; and of the third class, at the expiration of the sixth year; so that one-third may be chosen every second year; and if vacancies happen, by resignation or otherwise, during the recess of the legislature of any State, the executive thereof may make temporary appointments until the next meeting of the legislature, which shall then fill such vacancies.

No person shall be a senator who shall not have attained to the age of thirty years, and been nine years a citizen of the United States, and who shall not, when elected, be an inhabitant of that State for which he shall be chosen.

The vice-president of the United States shall be president of the senate, but shall have no vote unless they be equally divided.

The senate shall choose their other officers, and also a president *pro tempore*, in the absence of the vice-president, or when he shall exercise the office of president of the United States.

The senate shall have the sole power to try all impeachments; when sitting for that purpose, they shall be on oath or affirmation. When the president of the United States is tried, the chief justice shall preside; and no person shall be convicted without the concurrence of two-thirds of the members present.

Judgment, in cases of impeachment, shall not extend further than to removal from office, and disqualification to hold and enjoy any office of honor, trust, or profit, under the United States; but the party convicted shall nevertheless be liable and subject to indictment, trial, judgment, and punishment according to law.

SECT. 4. The times, places, and manner of holding elections for senators and representatives shall be prescribed in each State by the legislature thereof; but the Congress may at any time, by law, make or alter such regulations, except as to the places of choosing senators.

The Congress shall assemble at least once in every year; and such meeting shall be on the first Monday in December, unless they shall by law appoint a different day.

SECT. 5. Each house shall be the judge of the elections, returns, and qualifications of its own members; and a majority of each shall constitute a quorum to do business; but a smaller number may adjourn from day to day, and may be authorized to compel the attendance of absent members, in such manner, and under such penalties, as each house may provide.

Each house may determine the rules of its proceedings, punish its members for disorderly behavior, and, with the concurrence of two-thirds, expel a member.

Each house shall keep a journal of its proceedings, and from time to time publish the same, excepting such parts as may in their judgment require secrecy; and the yeas and nays of the members of either house on any question shall, at the desire of one-fifth of those present, be entered on the journal.

Neither house, during the session of Congress, shall, without the consent of the other, adjourn for more than three days, nor to any other place than that in which the two houses shall be sitting.

SECT. 6. The senators and representatives shall receive a compensation for their services, to be ascertained by law, and paid out of the treasury of the United States. They shall in all cases except treason, felony, and breach of the peace, be privileged from arrest during their attendance at the session of their respective houses, and in going to and returning from the same; and for any speech or debate in either house they shall not be questioned in any other place.

No senator or representative shall, during the time for which he was elected, be appointed to any civil office under the authority of the United States, which shall have been created, or the emoluments whereof shall have been increased, during such time; and no person holding any office under the United States shall be a member of either house during his continuance in office.

SECT. 7. All bills for raising revenue shall originate in the house of representatives; but the senate may propose or concur with amendments, as on other bills.

Every bill which shall have passed the house of representatives and the senate, shall, before it become a law, be presented to the president of the United States; if he approve, he shall sign it; but, if not, he shall return it, with his objections, to that house in which it shall have originated, who shall enter the objections at large on their journal, and proceed to reconsider it. If, after such reconsideration, two-thirds of that house shall agree to pass the bill, it shall be sent, together with the objections, to the other house, by which it shall likewise be reconsidered; and, if approved by two-thirds of that house, it shall become a law. But in all such cases the votes of both houses shall be determined by yeas and nays; and the names of the persons voting for and against the bill shall be entered on the journal of each house respectively. If any bill shall not be returned by the president within ten days (Sundays excepted) after it shall have been presented to him, the same shall be a law, in like manner as if he had signed it, unless the Congress, by their adjournment, prevent its return, in which case it shall not be a law.

Every order, resolution, or vote, to which the concurrence of the senate and house of representatives may be necessary (except on a question of adjournment), shall be presented to the president of the United States, and, before the same shall take effect, shall be approved by him; or, being disapproved by him, shall be re-passed by two-thirds of the senate and house of representatives, according to the rules and limitations prescribed in the case of a bill.

SECT. 8. The Congress shall have power to lay and collect taxes, duties, imposts, and excises, to pay the debts and provide for the common defence and general welfare of the United States; but all duties, imposts, and excises shall be uniform throughout the United States: to borrow money on the credit of the United States: to regulate commerce with foreign nations and among the several States, and with the Indian tribes: to establish an uniform rule of naturalization, and uniform laws on the subject of bankruptcies throughout the United States: to coin money, regulate the value thereof and of foreign coin, and fix the standard of weights and measures: to provide for the punishment of counterfeiting the securities and current coin of the United States: to establish post offices and post roads: to promote the progress of science and useful arts, by securing, for limited times, to authors and inventors, the exclusive right to their respective writings and discoveries: to constitute tribunals inferior to the supreme court: to define and punish piracies and felonies committed on the high seas, and offences against the law of nations: to declare war, grant letters of marque and reprisal, and make rules concerning captures on land and water: to raise and support armies; but no appropriation of money to that use shall be for a longer term than two years: to provide and maintain a navy: to make rules for the government and regulation of the land and naval forces: to provide for calling forth the militia to execute the laws of the Union, suppress insurrections, and repel invasions: to provide for organizing, arming, and disciplining the militia, and for governing such part of them as may be employed in the service of the United States; reserving to the States respectively the appointment of the officers, and the authority of training the militia according to the discipline prescribed by Congress: to exercise exclusive legislation in all cases whatsoever over such district (not exceeding ten miles square) as may by cession of particular States, and the acceptance of Congress, become the seat of the government of the United States; and to exercise like authority over all places purchased by the consent of the legislature of the State in which the same shall be, for the erection of forts, magazines, arsenals, dockyards, and other needful buildings: and to make all laws which shall be necessary and proper for carrying into execution the foregoing powers, and all other powers vested by this Constitution in the government of the United States, or in any department or officer thereof.

SECT. 9. The migration or importation of such persons as any of the States now existing shall think proper to admit shall not be prohibited by the Congress prior to the year one thousand eight hundred and eight; but a tax or duty may be imposed on such importation, not exceeding ten dollars for each person.

The privilege of the writ of *habeas corpus* shall not be suspended, unless when, in cases of rebellion or invasion, the public safety may require it.

No bill of attainder, or *ex post facto* law, shall be passed.

No capitation or other direct tax shall be laid, unless in proportion to the census, or enumeration, herein before directed to be taken.

No tax or duty shall be laid on articles exported from any State.

No preference shall be given, by any regulation of commerce or revenue, to the ports of one State over those of another; nor shall vessels bound to or from one State be obliged to enter, clear, or pay duties in another.

No money shall be drawn from the treasury but in consequence of appropriations made by law; and a regular statement and account of the receipts and expenditures of all public money shall be published from time to time.

No title of nobility shall be granted by the United States; and no person holding any office of profit or trust under them shall, without the consent of the Congress, accept of any present, emolument, office, or title, of any kind whatever, from any king, prince, or foreign state.

SECT. 10. No State shall enter into any treaty, alliance, or confederation; grant letters of marque and reprisal; coin money; emit bills of credit; make any thing but gold and silver coin a tender in payment of debts; pass any bill of attainder, *ex post facto* law, or law impairing the obligation of contracts; or grant any title of nobility. No State shall, without the consent of the Congress, lay any imposts, or duties, on imports or exports, except what may be absolutely necessary for executing its inspection laws; and the net produce of all duties and imposts, laid by any State on imports or exports, shall be for the use of the treasury of the United States; and all such laws shall be subject to the revision and control of the Congress. No State shall, without the consent of Congress, lay any duty of tonnage, keep troops, or ships of war, in time of peace, enter into any agreement or compact with another State or with a foreign power, or engage in war, unless actually invaded, or in such imminent danger as will not admit of delay.

ARTICLE II.

SECTION 1. The executive power shall be vested in a President of the United States of America. He shall hold his office during the term of four years; and, together with the Vice-President, chosen for the same term, be elected as follows: —

Each State shall appoint, in such manner as the legislature thereof may direct, a number of electors equal to the whole number of senators and representatives to which the State may be entitled in the Congress; but no senator or representative, or person holding an office of trust or profit under the Uuited States, shall be appointed an elector.

The electors shall meet in their respective States, and vote by ballot for two persons, of whom one, at least, shall not be an inhabitant of the same State with themselves: and they shall make a list of all the persons voted for, and of the number of votes for each, which list they shall sign and certify, and transmit, sealed, to the seat of the government of the United States, directed to the president of the senate. The president of the senate shall in the presence of the senate, and house of representatives, open all the certificates; and the votes shall then be counted. The person having the greatest number of votes shall be the president, if such number be a majority of the whole number of electors appointed; and if there be more than one who have such majority, and have an equal number of votes, then the house of representatives shall immediately choose by ballot one of them for president; and, if no person have a majority, then, from the five highest on the list, the said house shall, in like manner, choose the president: but, in choosing the president, the votes shall be taken by States, the representation from each State having one vote; a quorum for this purpose shall consist of a member or members from two-thirds of the States; and a majority of all the States shall be necessary to a choice. In every case, after the choice of the president, the person having the greatest number of votes of the electors shall be the vice-president. But, if there should remain two or more who have equal votes, the senate shall choose from them, by ballot, the vice-president. [See Amendments, Article XII.]

The Congress may determine the time of choosing the electors, and the day on which they shall give their votes; which day shall be the same throughout the United States.

No person, except a natural born citizen, or a citizen of the United States at the time of the adoption of this Constitution, shall be eligible to the office of president; neither shall any person be eligible to that office, who shall not have attained to the age of thirty-five years, and been fourteen years a resident within the United States.

In case of removal of the president from office, or of his death, resignation, or inability to discharge the powers and duties of the said office, the same shall devolve on the vice-president; and the Congress may by law provide for the case of removal, death, resignation, or inability both of the president and vice-president, declaring what officer shall then act as president; and such officer shall act accordingly, until the disability be removed, or a president shall be elected.

The president shall, at stated times, receive for his services a compensation, which shall neither be increased nor diminished during the period for which he shall have been elected; and he shall not receive, within that period, any other emolument from the United States, or any of them.

Before he enter on the execution of his office, he shall take the following oath or affirmation: —

"I do solemnly swear (or affirm) that I will faithfully execute the office of President of the United States, and will, to the best of my ability, preserve, protect, and defend the Constitution of the United States."

SECT. 2. The president shall be commander-in-chief of the army and navy of the United States, and of the militia of the several States, when called into the actual service of the United States. He may require the opinion, in writing, of the principal officer in each of the executive departments, upon any subject relating to the duties of their respective offices; and he shall have power to grant reprieves and pardons for offences against the United States, except in cases of impeachment.

He shall have power, by and with the advice and consent of the senate, to make treaties, provided two-thirds of the senators present concur; and he shall nominate, and, by and with the advice and consent of the senate, shall appoint, ambassadors, other public ministers and consuls, judges of the supreme court, and all other officers of the United States whose appointments are not herein otherwise provided for, and which shall be established by law; but the Congress may by law vest the appointment of such inferior officers as they think proper, in the president alone, in the courts of law, or in the heads of departments.

The president shall have power to fill up all vacancies that may happen during the recess of the senate, by granting commissions which shall expire at the end of their next session.

SECT. 3. He shall, from time to time, give to the Congress information of the state of the Union, and recommend to their consideration such measures as he shall judge necessary and expedient; he may, on extraordinary occasions, convene both houses, or either of them, and in case of disagreement between them, with respect to the time of adjournment, he may adjourn them to such time as he shall think proper; he shall receive ambassadors and other public ministers; he shall take care that the laws be faithfully executed, and shall commission all the officers of the United States.

SECT. 4. The president, vice-president, and all civil officers of the United States, shall be removed from office on impeachment for, and conviction of, treason, bribery, or other high crimes and misdemeanors.

ARTICLE III.

SECTION 1. The judicial power of the United States shall be vested in one supreme court, and in such inferior courts as the Congress may, from time to time, ordain and establish. The judges, both of the supreme and inferior courts, shall hold their offices during good behavior, and shall, at stated times, receive for their services a compensation, which shall not be diminished during their continuance in office.

SECT. 2. The judicial power shall extend to all cases in law and equity, arising under this Constitution, the laws of the United States, and treaties made, or which shall be made, under their authority; to all cases affecting ambassadors, other public ministers, and consuls; to all cases of admiralty and maritime jurisdiction; to controversies to which the United States shall be a party; to controversies between two or more States; between a State, and citizens of another State; between citizens of different States; between citizens of the same State claiming lands under grants of different States; and between a State, or the citizens thereof, and foreign states, citizens, or subjects. [See Amendments, Article XI.]

In all cases affecting ambassadors, other public ministers, and consuls, and those in which a State shall be a party, the supreme court shall have original jurisdiction. In all the other cases before mentioned, the supreme court shall have appellate jurisdiction, both as to law and fact, with such exceptions and under such regulations as the Congress shall make.

The trial of all crimes, except in cases of impeachment, shall be by jury; and such trial shall be held in the State where the said crimes shall have been committed; but, when not committed within any State, the trial shall be at such place or places as the Congress may by law have directed.

SECT. 3. Treason against the United States shall consist only in levying war against them, or in adhering to their enemies, giving them aid and comfort. No person shall be convicted of treason, unless on the testimony of two witnesses to the same overt act, or on confession in open court.

The Congress shall have power to declare the punishment of treason; but no attainder of treason shall work corruption of blood, or forfeiture, except during the life of the person attainted.

ARTICLE IV.

SECTION 1. Full faith and credit shall be given in each State to the public acts, records, and judicial proceedings of every other

State; and the Congress may, by general laws, prescribe the manner in which such acts, records, and proceedings shall be proved, and the effect thereof.

SECT. 2. The citizens of each State shall be entitled to all privileges and immunities of citizens in the several States.

A person charged in any State with treason, felony, or other crime, who shall flee from justice, and be found in another State, shall, on demand of the executive authority of the State from which he fled, be delivered up, to be removed to the State having jurisdiction of the crime.

No person held to service or labor in one State, under the laws thereof, escaping into another, shall, in consequence of any law or regulation therein, be discharged from such service or labor; but shall be delivered up on claim of the party to whom such service or labor may be due.

SECT. 3. New States may be admitted by the Congress into this Union; but no new State shall be formed or erected within the jurisdiction of any other State, nor any State be formed by the junction of two or more States or parts of States, without the consent of the legislatures of the States concerned, as well as of the Congress.

The Congress shall have power to dispose of, and make all needful rules and regulations respecting, the territory or other property belonging to the United States; and nothing in this Constitution shall be so construed as to prejudice any claims of the United States or of any particular State.

SECT. 4. The United States shall guarantee to every State in this Union a republican form of government; and shall protect each of them against invasion, and on application of the legislature, or of the executive (when the legislature cannot be convened), against domestic violence.

ARTICLE V.

The Congress, whenever two-thirds of both houses shall deem it necessary, shall propose amendments to this Constitution, or, on the application of the legislatures of two-thirds of the several States, shall call a convention for proposing amendments; which, in either case, shall be valid to all intents and purposes, as part of this Constitution, when ratified by the legislatures of three-fourths of the several States, or by conventions in three-fourths thereof, as the one or the other mode of ratification may be proposed by the Congress; provided, that no amendment which may be made prior to the year one thousand eight hundred and eight, shall, in any manner, affect the first and fourth clauses in the ninth section of the first article; and that no State, without its consent, shall be deprived of its equal suffrage in the senate.

ARTICLE VI.

All debts contracted, and engagements entered into before the adoption of this Constitution, shall be as valid against the United States under this Constitution, as under the confederation.

This Constitution, and the laws of the United States which shall be made in pursuance thereof, and all treaties made, or which shall be made, under the authority of the United States, shall be the supreme law of the land; and the judges in every State shall be bound thereby, any thing in the constitution or laws of any State to the contrary notwithstanding.

The senators and representatives before mentioned, and the members of the several State legislatures, and all executive and judicial officers, both of the United States and of the several States, shall be bound, by oath or affirmation, to support this Constitution; but no religious test shall ever be required as a qualification to any office or public trust under the United States.

ARTICLE VII.

The ratification of the conventions of nine States shall be sufficient for the establishment of this Constitution, between the States so ratifying the same.

AMENDMENTS.

ARTICLE I.

Congress shall make no law respecting an establishment of religion, or prohibiting the free exercise thereof; or abridging the freedom of speech, or of the press; or the right of the people peaceably to assemble, and to petition the government for a redress of grievances.

ARTICLE II.

A well-regulated militia being necessary to the security of a free state, the right of the people to keep and bear arms shall not be infringed.

ARTICLE III.

No soldier shall, in time of peace, be quartered in any house without the consent of the owner, nor in time of war but in a manner to be prescribed by law.

ARTICLE IV.

The right of the people to be secure in their persons, houses, papers, and effects, against unreasonable searches and seizures, shall not be violated; and no warrants shall issue, but upon probable cause, supported by oath or affirmation, and particularly describing the place to be searched, and the persons or things to be seized.

ARTICLE V.

No person shall be held to answer for a capital or otherwise infamous crime, unless on a presentment or indictment of a grand jury, except in cases arising in the land or naval forces, or in the militia when in actual service in time of war or public danger; nor shall any person be subject for the same offence to be twice put in jeopardy of life or limb; nor shall be compelled, in any criminal case, to be a witness against himself, nor be deprived of life, liberty, or property, without due process of law; nor shall private property be taken for public use, without just compensation.

ARTICLE VI.

In all criminal prosecutions, the accused shall enjoy the right to a speedy and public trial, by an impartial jury of the State and district wherein the crime shall have been committed, which district shall have been previously ascertained by law; and to be informed of the nature and cause of the accusation, to be confronted with the witnesses against him, to have compulsory process for obtaining witnesses in his favor, and to have the assistance of counsel for his defence.

ARTICLE VII.

In suits at common law, where the value in controversy shall exceed twenty dollars, the right of trial by jury shall be preserved; and no fact, tried by a jury, shall be otherwise re-examined, in any court of the United States, than according to the rules of the common law.

ARTICLE VIII.

Excessive bail shall not be required, nor excessive fines imposed, nor cruel and unusual punishments inflicted.

ARTICLE IX.

The enumeration, in the Constitution, of certain rights, shall not be construed to deny or disparage others retained by the people.

ARTICLE X.

The powers not delegated to the United States by the Constitution, nor prohibited by it, to the States, are reserved to the States respectively, or to the people.

ARTICLE XI.

The judicial power of the United States shall not be construed to extend to any suit in law or equity, commenced or prosecuted against one of the United States by citizens of another State, or by citizens or subjects of any foreign state.

ARTICLE XII.

The electors shall meet in their respective States, and vote by ballot for president and vice-president, one of whom, at least, shall not be an inhabitant of the same State with themselves; they shall name in their ballots the person voted for as president, aud in distinct ballots the person voted for as vice-president; and they shall make distinct lists of all persons voted for as president, and of all persons voted for as vice-president, and of the number of votes for each; which lists they shall sign and certify, and transmit sealed to the seat of the government of the United States, directed to the president of the senate. The president of the senate shall in the presence of the senate, and house of representatives, open all the certificates; and the votes shall then be counted; the person having the greatest number of votes for president shall be the president, if such number be a majority of the whole number of electors appointed: and, if no person have such majority, then from the persons having the highest numbers, not exceeding three, on the list of those voted for as president, the house of representatives shall choose immediately, by ballot, the president; but, in choosing the president, the votes shall be taken by States, the representation from each State having one vote; a quorum for this purpose shall consist of a member or members from two-thirds of the States, and a majority of all the States shall be necessary to a choice; and if the house of representatives shall not choose a president, whenever the right of choice shall devolve upon them, before the fourth day of March next following, then the vice-president shall act as president, as in the case of the death or other constitutional disability of the president.

The person having the greatest number of votes as vice-president shall be the vice-president, if such number be a majority of the whole number of electors appointed; and, if no person have a majority, then, from the two highest numbers on the list, the senate shall choose the vice-president; a quorum for the purpose shall consist of two-thirds of the whole number of senators; and a majority of the whole number shall be necessary to a choice.

But no person constitutionally ineligible to the office of president shall be eligible to that of vice-president of the United States.

ARTICLE XIII.

SECTION 1. Neither slavery nor involuntary servitude, except as a punishment for crime whereof the party shall have been duly convicted, shall exist within the United States, or any place subject to their jurisdiction.

SECT. 2. Congress shall have power to enforce this article by appropriate legislation.

ARTICLE XIV.

SECTION 1. All persons born or naturalized in the United States, and subject to the jurisdiction thereof, are citizens of the United States, and of the State wherein they reside. No State shall make or enforce any law which shall abridge the privileges or immunities of citizens of the United States; nor shall any State deprive any person of life, liberty, or property without due process of law, nor deny to any person within its jurisdiction the equal protection of the laws.

SECT. 2. Representatives shall be apportioned among the several States, according to their respective numbers, counting the whole number of persons in each State, excluding Indians not taxed. But when the right to vote at any election for the choice of electors for president and vice-president of the United States, representatives in Congress, the executive and judicial officers of a State, or the members of the legislature thereof, is denied to any of the male inhabitants of such State, being twenty-one years of age, and citizens of the United States, or in any way abridged, except for participation in rebellion or other crimes, the basis of representation shall be reduced in the proportion which the number of such male citizens shall bear to the whole number of male citizens, twenty-one years of age, in such State.

SECT. 3. No person shall be a senator or representative in Congress, or elector of president and vice-president, or hold any office, civil or military, under the United States or under any State, who having previously taken an oath as a member of Congress, or as an officer of the United States, or as a member of any State legislature, or as an executive or judicial officer of any State, to support the Constitution of the United States, shall have engaged in insurrection or rebellion against the same, or given aid or comfort to the enemies thereof. But Congress may by a vote of two-thirds of each house remove such disability.

SECT. 4. The validity of the public debt of the United States, authorized by law, including debts incurred for payment of pensions and bounties for services in suppressing insurrection or rebellion, shall not be questioned. But neither the United States, nor any State, shall assume or pay any debt or obligation incurred in aid of insurrection or rebellion against the United States, or any claim for the loss or emancipation of any slave; but all such debts, obligations, and claims shall be held illegal and void.

SECT. 5. The Congress shall have power to enforce by appropriate legislation the provisions of this article.

ARTICLE XV.

SECTION 1. The right of citizens of the United States to vote shall not be denied or abridged by the United States, or by any State, on account of race, color, or previous condition of servitude.

SECT. 2. The Congress shall have power to enforce this article by appropriate legislation.

INDEX.

INDEX.

Lightning Source UK Ltd.
Milton Keynes UK
UKHW020502070119
334942UK00007B/848/P